THE COMMONWEALTH

POLITICAL REALITIES
Edited on behalf of the Politics Association
by Bernard Crick and Derek Heater

Titles in the Series

POLITICAL REALITIES

The Commonwealth

Peter B. Harris

Longman

LONGMAN GROUP LIMITED
London
Associated companies branches and representatives
throughout the world

First published in 1975

ISBN 0 582 36628 3 (cased)
ISBN 0 582 36629 1 (paper)
Printed in Great Britain by Compton Printing Ltd., Aylesbury.

Contents

Acknowledgements

We are grateful to the following for permission to reproduce copyright material:
Associated Newspapers Group Ltd for the article 'Well, who wants this black and white show?' by John Dickinson from *London Evening News* 7th August, 1973; the author and Duke University Press for an extract from *The Open Commonwealth* by Professor M. Margaret Ball; Department of External Affairs, Canada for extracts from an address by Mr Marcel Cadieux, Canadian Ambassador to the United States to the International Relations Club Seattle 20th September, 1973 and extracts from an address by the Secretary of State for External Affairs the Hon. Mitchell Sharp to the Commonwealth Association of Architects, Ottawa 5th November 1973; Guardian Newspapers Ltd for an extract from the article 'Talking Heads' by Patrick Keatley in *The Guardian* 11th August, 1973 and the author and London Express News and Feature Services for an extract from the article 'All Smiles as Heath leaves for Cowes' by Robert Carvel in *Evening Standard* 9th August, 1973 and Times Newspapers Ltd for The Times Diary article 'Mr Wilson's nine day wonder from *The Times* 7th May 1975. Reprinted by permission of *The Times.*

Political Realities: the nature of the series

A great need is felt for short books which can supplement or even replace textbooks and which can deal in an objective but realistic way with problems that arouse political controversy. The series aims to break from a purely descriptive and institutional approach to one that will show how and why there are different interpretations both of how things work and how they ought to work. Too often in the past 'British Constitution' has been taught quite apart from any knowledge of the actual political conflicts which institutions strive to contain. So the Politics Association sponsors this new series because it believes that a specifically civic education is an essential part of any liberal or general education, but that respect for political rules and an active citizenship can only be encouraged by helping pupils, students and young voters to discover what the main objects are of political controversy, the varying views about the nature of the constitution—themselves often highly political—and what the most widely canvassed alternative policies are in their society. From such a realistic appreciation of differences and conflicts reasoning can then follow about the common processes of containing or resolving them peacefully.

The specific topics chosen are based on an analysis of the main elements in existing A level syllabuses, and the manner in which they are treated is based on the conviction of the editors that almost every examination board is moving, slowly but surely, away from a concentration on constitutional rules and towards a more difficult but important concept of a realistic political education or the enhancement of political literacy.

This approach has, of course, been common enough in the universities for many years. Quite apart from its civic importance, the teaching of politics in schools has tended to lag behind university practice and expectations. So the editors have aimed to draw on the most up-to-date academic knowledge, with some of the books being written by university teachers, some by secondary or further education teachers, but each group aware of the skills and knowledge of the other.

The Politics Association and the editors are conscious of the great importance of other levels of education, and are actively pursuing studies and projects of curriculum development in several directions, particularly towards CSE needs; but it was decided to begin with A level and new developments in sixth-form courses precisely because of the great overlap here between teaching in secondary schools and further education colleges, whether specifically for examinations or not; indeed most of the book will be equally useful for general studies.

Bernard Crick
Derek Heater

1 The Commonwealth

Critics of the British Empire . . . would have to admit that it is only half the truth to say that colonial freedom was extorted in the teeth of imperial obstruction; the other half is that it was latent in the imperial forms because they in turn were derived from a constitution moving towards freedom and that in the rhythm of ideas and of men liberalism and beneficence, if not continuous, were at least constantly recurrent.
Dame Margery Perham[1]

What is the Commonwealth?
The Commonwealth is an association of thirty-two independent states (1974) all of which have, at one time or another in the past been ruled by Great Britain. The Commonwealth is no longer an empire ruled by Britain, though it contains about fifteen territories which are still political dependencies of Great Britain. It is exceedingly difficult to define the Commonwealth any more precisely, and in order to show the diversity of thinking on the subject, we might perhaps consider some of the following descriptions, statements or comments:

The Legal. The Commonwealth consists of 'independent members [who] are fully sovereign states, having a status in international law no different from that of other sovereign states.'
Sir Ivor Jennings and C. H. Young, *Constitutional Laws of the Commonwealth,* (2nd edn, Oxford University Press, 1952) pp. 11-12

The Social. The Commonwealth is 'to be described most accurately in terms of an association or club'.
Arthur C. Turner, 'The Commonwealth: evolution or dissolution?' *Current History,* vol. 46, May 1964, p. 257.

The Satirical. The Commonwealth is 'the world's biggest experiment in sustained and creative historical humour . . . it has all the solidity that the frankly improbable so often acquires in human affairs'.
The Economist, 6, June, 1964, p. 1074

The Unbelieving. 'The British Commonwealth is an unclassifiable entity whose nature is outside the normal categories of political taxonomy.'
Turner, *op. cit.*

'The Commonwealth . . . is a farce . . . .'
'A Conservative', writing in *The Times,* 2 April, 1964.

The Composite. "A fraternal association", a "purely functional association", a "true cultural community", a "collection of nations associated for a few purposes but dissociated for most", a "loose international political entity", though not one comparable to other international organisms, "*sui generis*", and a British liability, perhaps the "concert of convenience" coined by Professor J. D. B. Miller comes closer than most to describing accurately the Commonwealth in its present incarnation.'
M. Margaret Ball analysing various descriptions of the Commonwealth in *The Open Commonwealth,* Duke University Press 1971, pp. 4-5.

The Commonwealth therefore may be regarded as a community of member states who belong to an international association which they are free to leave at any time.

For a political scientist the Commonwealth presents a number of problems. Let us consider some of them. Although the Commonwealth was in a sense a creation of British capacity for political innovation, the overwhelming majority of its inhabitants are not British, neither are they likely to want closer political ties with Great Britain in the future. Moreover the Commonwealth is the product of a combination of circumstances, partly historical and partly the result of conscious present day choice. The Commonwealth, while it created nothing, has been the means by which a large number of 'new' countries have come into existence. Thus, for example, British Acts of Parliament have been used to give effect to the independence of 'old colonies' as 'new states'. Somewhat paradoxically the British, proud possessors of a 'non-written' constitution, have been prolific creators of a written constitution for others.[2]

The Commonwealth too has made possible the emergence of many new nation-states, although what the exact boundaries of these new nation-states are or ought to be has not always been an easy question to determine.

A useful way to approach the political meaning of the Commonwealth would be to look at it in terms of certain apparently negative factors. The truth is that the Commonwealth is a quasi-political device which is easier to explain in terms of what it is *not* rather than what it is. Let us consider what we do not find in it. We note:

1 The absence of a central law-making body or federal parliament which might be expected to serve as sovereign (although a severely restricted higher court of appeal exists known as the Judicial Committee of the Privy Council).

2 The absence of a single common head apart from a purely nominal title held by the Queen: Head of the Commonwealth. A further paradox derives from the existence of a large number of republics within the Commonwealth. A body which retains a monarch even as its nominal Head suggests some overall attachment to the monarchical spirit. In fact, since the independence of India in 1947, the republican principle has been accepted.[3]

3 The absence of any common ethnic or cultural bond between its members overall. In some respects the cultural bond is evidently strong, as between Britain and New Zealand, or between the various Indian, Chinese or African communities. In many cases different communities frequently find themselves involved in conflict, as in the cases of Chinese and Malays in Malaysia, Hindu and Muslim in India, or French and English-speaking Canadians, Tamils and Singhalese in Sri Lanka, and various tribes in Africa. Indeed the Commonwealth is everywhere beset with sectional communal and tribal politics. Of course, these conflicts exist outside the Commonwealth too, and they have led in some measure, for example in the case of Eire and South Africa, to the withdrawal of these particular states from the Commonwealth connection.

So far then, we have suggested that the Commonwealth is full of puzzles, problems and paradoxes. This manner of reasoning is unsatisfactory and no doubt most people would want to discuss the subject in a less negative fashion. Many statesmen and politicians within the Commonwealth use phrases such as Commonwealth 'partnership', 'connection', 'link', which sometimes appears to suggest that there is a structured association of states which somehow collectively constitutes some form of coherent whole.[4] There is, however, no structured Commonwealth association, whatever platitudes may be uttered by particular politicians from time to time. If, however, we attempt to organise a few more positive ideas on the subject we might argue that the Commonwealth does in fact perform certain fairly well defined functions.

1 It functions as an administrative unit, particularly since the creation in 1967 of the Commonwealth Secretariat. The Commonwealth operates through a vast network of cooperative committees which have been developed in order to organise the many inter-Commonwealth services. For example, in the fields of education, agriculture, health, there is a great deal of cooperation in various ways for various purposes.
2 It functions as a vast area of interest whose size ensures a market both large and diverse. Here the very size of the Commonwealth can be deceptive: it is not a power bloc, but rather an association, though this element is sometimes misunderstood by many outsiders. In economic terms, for example, the commonwealth has in the past given preference to trade between member nations, and this fact alone has been adequate to give coherence to the Commonwealth bond.
3 The Commonwealth has further developed and continued to survive because it serves a need. No state is forced to join it and no state is required to belong to the Commonwealth should it not wish to do so. Hence membership, being a voluntary act, depends on calculations made by the individual member. Generally each member state calculates that membership carries with it greater advantages than disadvantages. It therefore chooses to remain a member for reasons which are normally primarily economic. However, to put it crudely, states normally belong to the Commonwealth because such membership gives them both status and protection in an uncertain world. To withdraw from the Commonwealth implies no new status and suggests that protection is available only from the superpowers, Which in turn suggests the exchange of one colonial ruler for another. The Commonwealth, however, does not maintain a comprehensive defence treaty between its various members. Indeed some of them have concluded alliances with various external powers which are hostile to each other, the case for example between India

and Pakistan, while on several occasions serious wars have been fought between various Commonwealth countries.

4 The Commonwealth further gives rise to a need for what might be called publicity, the publicising or making known the existence of a state which might otherwise never be able to gain adequate knowledge or recognition of its existence let alone its activities. It is clear that certain small states can gain recognition only by belonging to an organisation which may perhaps magnify their power. When chided by some 'anti-colonial' powers because of their continued membership of the Commonwealth, on the grounds that the Commonwealth was not revolutionary enough perhaps some states have in mind the reported reply of Voltaire on his deathbed that it was then no time to make unnecessary enemies.

The more positive aspects of the Commonwealth, then, may be summarised as: *organisation, size, need* and *publicity*. This does not exhaust our statement of the problem because there are still moments when these positive factors are possibly potentially divisive. A large organisation, for example, will often produce its own problems. Indeed we may examine the Commonwealth from another perspective and say that the association operates as long as those forces which hold it together outweigh those which tend to draw it apart. We might further put this by saying that the Commonwealth contains both the forces of fusion as well as the forces of fission. On the whole the forces which tend to weaken split or divide the Commonwealth are political, or perhaps more accurately political-ideological, while those which tend to strengthen it are more likely to be economic, though such categories are often artificial if economic difficulties develop which take on political overtones.

A good example of the general proposition that political-ideological factors are elements of potential disruption may be discerned from the debate over the withdrawal of South Africa in 1961.[5] As South Africa refused to modify its internal racial policies, many Commonwealth countries refused to trade with her or even to accept her within the group. Economic measures were here employed to further a political end.

Any economic coherence that the Commonwealth may have is largely due to the fact that Britain built up the old Empire in order to make the parts into some sort of economic whole. This is true in India,

Australia, most parts of Africa, the Caribbean and South-east Asia. It is clearly of some advantage to create larger economic and political blocs rather than have small largely autonomous areas proliferating without proper cohesion.

Particular events and developments have often had profound effects on Commonwealth relations, and have made them in a sense more fragile and more brittle. However healthy the Commonwealth might be at any particular time it is possible that some unforeseen issue might emerge which would imply great difficulties for the association. In recent years the Commonwealth has been put under severe strain by many international issues which it is not equipped to solve. The Cold War, the Rhodesian Independence issue, the problems of the Indian sub-continent, for example, have all placed enormous strains on its structure and hence threatened its very survival. That the Commonwealth still survives is a tribute to its basic strength. It has survived, in fact, because it never had any formal rules to break. The only rule is that in the process of decision-making a broad agreement should be accepted by all its members (though after all the points at issue have been thoroughly debated), subject only to the final drastic action of withdrawal on the part of any state which cannot tolerate the decision reached. The final sanction is withdrawal from the Commonwealth.[6]

Commonwealth principles

We might reasonably ask the question for what principles does the Commonwealth stand? An answer to the question might stress human rights, dignity, trust, mutual tolerance, but while some of these things are undoubtedly present, it would be wrong to see a clear and comprehensive statement of principles implied in Commonwealth membership. There are no moral or categorical imperatives.

On the whole it is more correct to see the Commonwealth as a morally neutral organisation except in one very important particular. The exception would appear to be the case of race relations. All members pay lip-service to an essentially negative 'principle', which may be expressed as an abhorrence of apartheid. At the Commonwealth Conference held at Singapore in 1971 an attempt was made to introduce a more systematic statement of this dislike on the basis of a set of principles designed to outlaw racial discrimination.[7] If such a declaration of principles had been drawn up a Commonwealth Bill of Rights would have been created, together with sanctions and penalties not excluding expulsion for non-compliance.

The notion of a declaration of Commonwealth principles was not accepted by Britain and certain other countries. Britian did not wish to be tied to any form of ideological commitment; such a notion was anathema to the British Prime Minister, (Edward Heath), In the end the Conference accepted a 'Commonwealth Declaration' which stated general support for the principles of liberty, equality, fraternity and self-determination.

The significance of the proposal to write a system of Commonwealth principles would have been very great, particularly if accompanied by a corresponding system of penalties for non-compliance. In the first place those who advocate such a declaration might find themselves, inadvertently or otherwise, accused for infringing these elevated principles. Human nature being what it is, those states which are subjected to such penalties will always seek to apply their logic to those who make the accusation.

In the second place a declaration of principles could clearly make a great deal of difference to the workings of an association whose very nature and existence has always been essentially informal. Originally the Commonwealth Prime Ministers simply met together in a social gathering, taking no formal decisions, but seeking rather a like-minded approach to matters of common concern. They spoke, as it were, the same language.

There is no intrinsic merit in the excessive informality of earlier days which has for so long prevailed in Commonwealth relationships. It is quite possible to have a relationship between a handful of like-minded elder statesmen which could successfully operate as it did when perhaps four or five 'old' dominions,* met together possibly coincidentally with Test matches in view.

However, in the new complicated era of Commonwealth negotiations in which thirty-three highly disparate and sometimes self-concious states are involved, there is some case to be made for a statement of intent. The difficulty which attaches to the publication of such a view lies partly in the content of the proposed declaration and partly in the nature of the penalties, if any, proposed for non-compliance. It is therefore highly unlikely that any comprehensive statement of Commonwealth philosphy and policy can ever effectively be made. The question

* Dominion status is discussed in Chapter 2.

which arises relates to the nature of what might be called the Commonwealth 'drift'. For long the Commonwealth has appeared to move without a particular purpose in a manner which may perhaps suit the native British temperament, but may be highly unsatisfactory otherwise. One might legitimately wonder however whether an association can flourish without purpose or organisation (*pace* the Commonwealth Secretariat). In fact the protagonists of the Declaration of Principles view have a great deal of substance in their case. The Commonwealth is unlikely to drift permanently without captain, navigator or compass, apart from establishing the most basic degree of communication. At some time or other certain states will break away when the tenuous bonds which hold together finally snap as in the cases of South Africa and Pakistan.

The statement of principles which are frequently intended to shape a future Commonwealth might perhaps contain a statement that any Commonwealth state might bring an action against any other Commonwealth state which infringes certain basic human norms. There is, however, at present no machinery by which an 'offending' nation can be brought to account for its actions. The nearest equivalent may be the Judicial Committee of the Privy Council, which is the highest Court of Appeal for a number of states as well as for the remaining colonies. The Judicial Committee has jurisdiction with regard to individuals not states, but no doubt it could be turned into a Supreme Court to adjudicate cases brought against particular states for infringements of the Commonwealth code.

Such a code, if adopted, might operate according to two principles: it might outlaw all official actions within any country which discriminates against any one group; and it might forbid any action designed to cause permanent economic damage against any member state.

In practical terms what many of the new states require is a statement of determined opposition to South African apartheid (as well as its Rhodesian variant) coupled with a determination and preparedness to use strong punitive measures to terminate it. A more generalised statement would be much more difficult to formulate because of the difficulty of defining such terms and 'oppression' or 'discrimination'. Within many Commonwealth states there are minority groups which protest that their rights are constantly infringed – such language rights as in Canada, religious rights as in Sri Lanka and those of

Indian businessmen in Uganda and Kenya. A consequence of a half-hearted or illogical application of principles might be that certain states could be accused of 'selective indignation'. To put this another way, it might be argued that some states could be viewed as sharpening swords which could be turned against themselves.

The dilemma which has faced the Commonwealth for some time is that it requires a more precise definition of aims and objectives yet does not require a programme so precise that it becomes a strangulating ideology. The Commonwealth requires a lead not a bridle.

The Commonwealth Secretariat 1965

As early as 1903 proposals were advanced to create a Secretariat to organise the handling of the affairs of the Commonwealth.[8] These proposals did not succeed, either because of opposition from Commonwealth members or because it was felt that, in true British style, informality and friendly consultation between the Old Commonwealth members was an adequate means of conducting the business of the association. With the advent of new states to the Commonwealth the need for better administrative procedures became more evident.

In 1960 the Commonwealth contained eleven members, which was almost too many to be accommodated in the Cabinet Room at No. 10, Downing Street. In the next eight years seventeen members were added. The old informality became impossible, and a regular machinery was required to increase the efficiency of the Commonwealth arrangements, play a useful part between the governments and act as a public relations organisation for the member nations of the Commonwealth. The Secretariat was finally established in 1965 and Arnold Smith of Canada was made the first Secretary-General.

The creation of the Commonwealth Secretariat in 1965 had two important implications for the founding member of the Commonwealth.

1 The role of Britain as coordinator and administrator of the Commonwealth became reduced. Since the beginning of the Commonwealth, the structure of the organisation was what was determined by the most senior member, Britain. Further, with the dismantling of the old Commonwealth Office, many functions were transferred to the new Secretariat.
2 The functioning of the Commonwealth itself changed in a significant way. The Commonwealth now developed its own organisation which

could make appropriate arrangements. While preparations for Commonwealth Prime Minister conferences were the most important task, most of the Secretariat work was of a routine nature.

The Commonwealth Secretary-General, Arnold Smith did not, however, regard the office as a mere exercise in public administration. His first annual report, published in 1966, stated that 'the Commonwealth is a living organism, not a political blueprint'.

Organisation and relationships

Although the Commonwealth has not formulated any precise ideological programme it would be wrong to conclude that it has no working 'rules'. Even here, we must proceed with a great deal of caution. It must be stressed that the Commonwealth is unlikely to be able to set out these 'rules' in any detail, but, perhaps we might specify the following points in this connection.

1 All Commonwealth states are autonomous entities in no way subject to the wishes or dictates of other members. In practice, of course, governments are at liberty to accept or reject any line of argument put forward by other member states, to enter into working arrangements, groups or blocs as the issue under discussion requires. In practice, too, the Commonwealth has tended to divide into two sections consisting on the one hand of the relatively richer white and the poorer Afro-Asian-Caribbean members. Canada has frequently identified itself more closely, in terms of its ideological commitment, with the Third World than have any of the former Dominions.
2 The Commonwealth depends upon individual states and not on any organisational machinery for the implementation of its decisions. There is no such notion as majority rule attaching to the formulation of decisions and resolutions. However, prior to the taking of any decision or resolution much discussion and debate will take place in groups and cabals.
3 The Commonwealth operates in an apparently *ad hoc* manner and this is the fundamental point to remember about the 'international relations' of the Commonwealth, stemming as it does from Commonwealth autonomy. In many respects, however, there is a need to associate the various communities, and a continuous secretarial and governmental liaison operates on a practical level. The large members of committees and administrative organs which link up the many

Commonwealth agencies have been coordinated into the Commonwealth Secretariat.

The Commonwealth is of course an association and has often been described as unique, which could never consciously have been created. Sir Kenneth Wheare once said that, 'if the Commonwealth did not exist, it would be impossible to create'. It has come into being as a product of British imperial history and is unlikely to be repeated at any other time or place. This is not to say that its members could not or do not join other associations. Any state can ally or associate itself with any group within or outside the Commonwealth body. Some of these other associations to which Commonwealth countries give their support and allegiance are religious in character, such as the Muslim League to which Pakistan and Malaysia have belonged as well as certain non-Commonwealth Muslim states in the Middle East. Britain herself belongs to many non-Commonwealth associations such as the North Atlantic Treaty Organisation (NATO), the South-East Asian Treaty Organisation (SEATO), the Central Treaty Association (CENTO), the United Nations, and most significantly of all, the European Economic Community from 1973.

It may be something of a surprise that Britain has for long belonged to military organisations without this involving any comment on the part of her Commonwealth partners. Her membership of the European Economic Community has evoked much more comment. In 1971, at the Commonwealth Prime Minister's Conference held at Singapore, the British Prime Minister, Edward Heath, reasserted what he described as British rights, stating that he reserved freedom of action for Great Britain to adopt any policies which were felt to be in her own national interest. Before that time there had been a tendency for Britain to act as a catalyst or a cipher in Commonwealth matters, rarely taking the initiative but tending rather to wait on events.

Each member state of the Commonwealth must make whatever calculations it can regarding its continued membership. Relatively few states have left the Commonwealth. Those that have done so have believed (or at least their leaders at that particular point in time have believed) that their interests have best been served outside the Commonwealth. Burma's departure reflected a national identity outside. Eire's effective departure in 1937 reflected that country's dissatisfaction with British policy, not unconnected with three centuries of Anglo-

Irish conflict; it was at least as much an anti-British gesture as a constructive action, for Southern Ireland had been an independent Dominion since 1922. South Africa's departure in 1961 was an inevitable consequence of the South African election of 1948 which brought the Nationalist Afrikaner party to power: the doctrine of apartheid became established orthodoxy not only for Afrikaners but also for many English-speaking South Africans. The new non-white Commonwealth members refused to accept South Africa's continuing candidature, and the South African Prime Minister, Dr Verwoerd announced that South Africa would leave the Commonwealth. Pakistan's departure in 1972 came at the end of its war with India and the loss of its eastern section, which became established as the new state of Bangladesh. Pakistan's intention was to demonstrate its profound dissatisfaction with India which had become involved in the attempt of (West) Pakistan to punish secession of (East) Pakistan, leading to the creation of the state of Bangladesh. In some respects this again was no more than a gesture, but given Pakistan's defeat, the attendant horrors of the war and the dismemberment of that country, not to mention the deep bitterness between the two states, Pakistan had little alternative if she wished to give some strong indication of dismay at the loss of East Pakistan. However, as Pakistan terminated her Commonwealth association so Bangladesh applied for membership, making her calculations that the value of Commonwealth membership was preferable to a state of isolation.

The case of Bangladesh may throw some light on the reasons why states seek Commonwealth membership. In the uncertain world of international politics most states require to enter into some form of alliance with a large group – in practical terms with some major power or powers. During the Cold War epoch following the Second World War the international community assumed a simple bipolar division between those in either the Soviet or the American sphere of influence. The Commonwealth was a much more innocent structure, with basically non-military implications, but, its lack of weight in the *realpolitik world* of international politics did not make it less attractive to the new states of Africa and Asia. From 1956 onwards it was forced to find formulas to reduce its suggestion of being no more than Old Empire in new form. It was of course incomprehensible to foreigners who saw it as a continuation of the influence of Whitehall after granting of a pseudo-independence.

However, the Commonwealth did remain viable and its members remained faithful. Without this fidelity the members of the Commonwealth would long since have disappeared from the international scene. The fidelity exits even when the smaller Commonwealth state is apparently threatened by a larger bloc, state or grouping. One might consider states such as Lesotho, Gibraltar, Canada and Hong Kong as examples in this important category. Each of these is strongly influenced by a powerful non-Commonwealth neighbour which might, without this membership of the Commonwealth, make a *de facto* absorption of the less powerful neighbour. Thus Lesotho is an enclave within, and largely dependent on, South Africa, Gibraltar is an appendage of Spain, Canada is in many ways an appendage of the USA and Hong Kong is culturally Chinese, retaining its existence only at the discretion of China, and in any case terminating its lease in 1997.

In order to appreciate the contrast between membership and non-membership consider the position of any one small Afro-Asian member of the Commonwealth. It enjoys its particular status with the international community because its voice can be heard within and as part of the Commonwealth; outside the Commonwealth it would be both vulnerable and probably ignored. The most useful contrasting analogy would be to mention the case of Japan, which is friendless in the area of East Asia. Japan has been forced to establish its position purely on the basis of its strength and alliances. Despite its vast and growing wealth, Japan was profoundly shocked by the American initiative towards China in 1971. Accepting their protection from 1945 onwards, Japan was content to let the United States dominate its foreign policy. When President Nixon visited China, Japan, virtually uninformed of the visit, discovered that it had no comparable Commonwealth partners whom it could consult. It was, at that time, virtually friendless. Japan's only sensible move during 1971-72 was to prepare the way, and to move from a dependence on an alliance with one superpower to an understanding with another. Commonwealth members are free to be friendless, but as there is no cost to be permanently established on a vast consultative network involving more than thirty nations over all the continents, it is not surprising that most countries choose to belong rather than to remove themselves.

From time to time private remarks are made that there are two Commonwealths, not one. The first consists of the original colonies of settlers from Great Britain itself who created communities or 'plantations' of settlers in the new world in the seventeenth century. In some cases not all the settlers were of British origin, and this led to certain complications. Canada became British in the eighteenth century and remained loyal to the Crown after the American Revolution of 1776. Canada was originally a French possession during the seventeenth century, but was 'lost' to the British as a result of the Treaty of Paris 1763, and Quebec became a British possession in 1773. Quebec was the area in which the French Canadians had principally settled. The second example is South Africa, originally Dutch, but captured by the British in 1802 during the French Revolutionary Wars. The Dutch settlers never accepted British rule and trekked deep into the African hinterland to escape British dominion, thus coming into contact (and conflict) with African tribes in the interior. In both Canada and South Africa the pattern of settlement was disturbed as one partner attempted to dominate the other. In South Africa the position was further complicated by rivalries between African tribes and, later, by the inflow of Indian workers to the sugar plantations of Natal.

New Zealand (paradoxically, in view of its Dutch-sounding name) presents a less complicated example. British norms predominate because, unlike Canada and South Africa, only one white racial group (of British origin) has settled there. In a survey taken in 1972 it was revealed that as many as 60 per cent of New Zealanders would qualify for a British passport if this were to be given on the basis of having a British grandparent. Australia's case, while similar to that of New Zealand differs in the sense that her recent influx of 'New Australians' – a term used to describe immigrants of non-British origin such as Greeks, Italians, and Yugoslavs is gradually producing a new ethnic amalgam.

However, neither New Zealand nor Australia is yet at ease in the Pacific region in which they coexist. The dilemma results from the fact that both New Zealand and Australia will always be *in* but not *of* Asia. The ties of British ancestry, culture and attachment are possibly less meaningful than they were, and it is true to say that the Old Commonwealth is slowly drifting away from the British connection in all but the cultural essentials. The case of English-speaking South Africa clearly brings out the deep sense of loss which they suffer when they are separated from the British cultural ethos: the sense of loss of contact between Great Britain and the Old Dominions is strong. English-speaking South Africans have retained a strong attachment to their English cultural norms, in spite of the competing dominance of

Afrikaner culture. In the case of Rhodesia we can perhaps speak of a white African nationalism in the sense of the development of a rival strength to black African nationalism, but this nationalism is still no more than a deviant from its parent in Europe. Rhodesia's rebellion has been anti-Black but not anti-British. Even after the unilateral declaration of independence in 1965, Rhodesian attachment to British habits and standards remained generally unquestioned. Rhodesian national awareness, the root cause of UDI may be an excellent example of the comment made by Sir Isaiah Berlin that 'nationalism is an inflamed condition of national consciousness'. It is the presence of a rival Black nationalism which has inflamed white Rhodesians.

The New Commonwealth is easily recognised; its major characteristics are that it is non-white, poor and generally the result of British conquest, annexation, and colonisation during centuries past. The New Commonwealth is almost entirely situated in Africa, Asia and the Caribbean. All the New Commonwealth states have gained independence since 1947 and most of them since 1960. Some of them like India had been under British rule for three hundred years prior to independence. Others like Tanzania had been ruled by Britain only since 1918. Many of them were suspicious of the white members of the club because of their empathy one for the other. The original Commonwealth members were often out of sympathy with the approach of the new members who desired to give priority to such questions as the removal of white minority rule in Southern Africa, the problems of underdevelopment and migration within the Commonwealth. Gradually as the numbers of Commonwealth members grew from five in 1946 to thirty-three in 1973, so the influence of the New Commonwealth grew stronger. Although the Commonwealth did not take decisions in terms of votes it tended to divide into blocs and groups. The most important questions of course related to Africanisation, the pace of independence and the status of Africans still living in areas in which political power still remained entrenched in 'white hands'.

So far we have discussed various definitions of the Commonwealth, trying to see what it means. We must now try to tackle a far more difficult question, namely what people think the Commonwealth means. There are, as might be imagined, a large number of different interpretations to be considered. For the sake of simplicity, however, we suggest three approaches to this difficult problem; the sceptical, the optimistic and the pragmatic. It must be stressed that these are essentially British interpretations because it would be difficult to make the analysis from the standpoint of every Commonwealth country. The interpretations which follow are presented as a basis for discussion. An illustration of each, drawn from newspaper reports of the Commonwealth Prime Ministers' Conference of August 1973, is provided in appendix D.

The sceptics. Those who see the Commonwealth either as a loosely structured unworkable association, or as a hollow mockery may be described as the Commonwealth sceptics. There are very many sceptics both in Britain and elsewhere and they are inclined to repeat the famous charge of an anonymous writer in *The Times* that the Commonwealth is a 'farce', There is, behind this charge, a straightforward rationale. The argument of the sceptics is one of *realpolitik.* It suggests that .the Commonwealth is a disparate, ungainly, unwieldy monstrosity with a perverse attachment to double standards. The New Commonwealth countries in particular appear to be saying, 'Do what I say' rather than 'Do what I do', Those countries in particular which inveigh against misgovernment, inhuman repression and discriminatory laws in particular Commonwealth countries, jealously preserve their own rights regarding freedom of action in internal affairs. The sceptics believe that the many attacks on apartheid, however well justified, come ill from countries which practise less publicised but perhaps equally pernicious forms of oppression and discrimination.

The sceptics regard this 'selective indignation' as a form of hypocrisy which is unfortunately endemic within the Commonwealth. Thus India would not accept external criticism of her caste system, of her forcible seizure of Goa, of her Kashmiri or Naga policy, nor even of any guilt regarding her 1962 war with China. The sceptics would argue that the policy of India has long betrayed a double standard. The many states in Africa which have set up single party states or military dictatorships have, wittingly or unwittingly practised forms of repression and discrimination all the worse for not being openly publicised and discussed. Uganda too, which under Dr Obote vociferously attacked British policy, including British Rhodesian policy, demonstrated, with its eviction, mistreatment and deportation of Asians that it was far more cruelly racialist than any of those whom it attacked in this respect.

The sceptics further question the value of the Commonwealth on the ground that it is an association of highly disparate states, races and nations. They believe that the ties of blood and kinship are paramount in any sort of association. The Old Commonwealth is therefore tenable purely on a kinship basis and is meaningful only in so far as like speak to like. The expanded and extended Commonwealth is seen as an impossible attempt to merge into one association, a vast heterogeneous mass of unrelated, unconnected races, groups and nations which spend their time in wishful thinking about their aims and objects but which produce no more than a 'tale of sound and fury signifying nothing'. The British Queen should be the Commonwealth's Queen and any Republic should remove itself or be removed.

Sceptics may perhaps most often be found amongst some members and former members of the Conservative Party, most particularly on the right wing. Their spokesman is sometimes Enoch Powell, and members of the Monday Club (a section of the Party expressing strongly 'conservative' views) are decidedly hostile to many of the new states of the Commonwealth; there are probably many other but less strident sceptics in Britain. The Commonwealth is not a question which arouses a great deal of enthusiasm in Britain generally, except in the form of Commonwealth immigration, and British workers are probably apathetic about the subject. Those British residents who are likely to know something about the Commonwealth are former members of the Colonial Service. When independence has curtailed their careers they may be sceptical or even hostile to the Commonwealth. They may write letters to the newspapers expressing views or relating experiences which may have some effect upon policy makers. They are at least articulate on the subject.

A final group of importance who are sometimes sceptical about the Commonwealth are the advocates of 'Europeanism', as against the continued Commonwealth connection. To the extent that Europeans in all British political parties place their first priority on the cause of European integration, they must necessarily tend to discount the Commonwealth. The Marketeers, as they are known, will of course deny any belittling of the Commonwealth, but most Commonwealth members fail to see the logic of the Marketeers in so far as this is injurious to them, nor do they appreciate statements to the effect that British entry will not cause them economic damage.

The sceptics are without doubt a powerful group, believing that when the Empire was 'liquidated' to use Professor Carrington's term, it remained 'liquidated'.[9] The Commonwealth is not to be regarded as a true successor to the British Empire, because it is neither British nor a true Commonwealth of nations. The sceptics refuse to be a party to the 'farce'.

The optimists. The optimists do not accept what they regard as the essentially negative and pessimistic interpretation of the sceptics. The Commonwealth is for them a great multiracial experiment, one which can never be repeated. Much of the rhetoric used about the former Empire is used by the modern enthusiasts for the Commonwealth, such as its description as a great Family or Brotherhood of Nations. Lloyd George is on record in 1907 as describing the Commonwealth as a 'Federation of Free Commonwealths', and Sir Wilfred Laurier described it in 1908 as a 'galaxy of independent nations'. Perhaps the heights of plauditry were employed by Sir Robert Menzies, Australian Prime Minister, who spoke of it (the then British Empire) as 'a tang in the air; a touch of salt on the lips; a little pulse that beats and shall beat; a decent pride; a sense of continuing city'. And again; 'Unless the British Empire is to British people all over the world a spirit, a proud memory, a confident prayer, courage for the future, it is nothing.'*

The Commonwealth, say the optimists, is to be seen as the only genuine association of peoples from all over the world, transcending boundaries of class, race and religion. They argue that its power for good is incalculable, and it could be the means for a genuine cooperation between like-minded peoples everywhere. What they see as remarkable is not the differences which separate the divergent groups within it but rather the continued existence of the Commonwealth. One might point to the great difficulties (not to mention a multiplicity of coups) which have beset it, whether deriving from Rhodesia, India and Pakistan, Malaysia, Cyprus, Kenya, Nigeria or Uganda. In spite of these problems the Commonwealth has survived, with very few signs that it is about to liquidate itself. The optimists of course recognise that new issues will arise from time to time which will subject the Commonwealth to severe stresses and strains. Judging by past experience, however, they feel that the future is secure because, given goodwill and a basic desire to maintain the association, no problem of future Commonwealth relations is too difficult.

The secession of South Africa in 1961 was, for the optimists, an

* The Rt. Hon. R. G. Menzies, addressing the Australian Institute of International Affairs, Adelaide, 26 June, 1950.

act of great importance because it removed from the Commonwealth the one state which legally enshrined permanent racial inequality in its internal policy. South Africa appeared to be a totally unacceptable member of the Commonwealth, three-quarters of whose peoples were non-white. Some optimists argued that the case of Uganda, which expelled its Asian residents in 1972, was rather different from that of South Africa. Initially Uganda sought to expel Asians who held British passports and were therefore regarded as non-citizens for whom Britain should accept responsibility. The Ugandan action, they felt, need not necessarily be construed as overtly racial, though there was some debate about this point, and some optimists felt uneasy because double standards in such matters should be avoided. No urgent meeting of the Commonwealth was called in 1972, as it had been over Rhodesia in 1966, and many optimists as well as Commonwealth members regarded the matter as serious but by no means fatal. The optimists' use of intuition rather than logic may be justified by their knowledge that the majority of the members of the Commonwealth would accept the correctness of South Africa's removal but would not endorse an equal censure on (not to mention explusion of) Uganda.

If the optimists were to be asked to stand up and be counted they would include those of liberal persuasion (including many members of the Liberal Party) but also including many members of the Labour party, more particularly those of middle-class background. The Labour Party's stand on this matter is of some interest and may be briefly assessed here. While the Labour Party waited for office, particularly during the years preceding the Second World War, it appeared to oppose the Empire partly because it was out of harmony with the conception of an international socialist brotherhood, and partly because they regarded it as an agency of international capitalism and exploitation. The Labour Party came into office in 1945 and India gained independence in 1947 after about three hundred years of British administration. Step by step, and with the growth of the New Commonwealth, the Labour Party came to look on the new body as a praiseworthy association of free peoples, referring to it in phraseology similar to that earlier employed by Conservatives about the Empire. The Conservatives on the other hand, were relatively unenthusiastic about the New Commonwealth, though they had been, since the time of Disraeli, the party of Empire. The Labour Party which had been hostile to the Empire, became tender to the New Commonwealth.

There was moreover considerable support for the optimists' cause in certain parts of Whitehall. Many Colonial Office officials as well as Commonwealth Relations Office staff, and later the Commonwealth section of the Foreign and Commonwealth Office, made prodigious efforts to make independence operations a success. These efforts involved giving assistance, moral and financial, to the new states as well as taking the initiative in devising constitutions, legal systems and forms of local government in many cases. The prototype of the new Colonial civil servant was Sir Andrew Cohen, head of the African division at the Colonial Office, who gained a reputation for his liberal thinking on Africa and who became a Governor of Uganda about ten years before independence. Cohen wrote a book[10] on the changing Africa which he portrayed as a hopeful venture. However, African political consciousness was now awakened and a growing hostility to British rule led to a clash between Britain and the Kabaka (or King) of the province of Buganda.[11] The Kabaka was exiled in 1953 after Cohen had taken many steps to introduce 'large-scale progressive reforms', but also after a bitter constitutional conflict. What Cohen had done was to develop certain 'representative national institutions and democratic local government', albeit late in the day. Given the subsequent history of much of Black Africa, there is some reason to believe that the optimists have not been cautious enough in tempering their dreams to reality.

The pragmatists. The pragmatists are those who see the Commonwealth as a sensible proposition as long as it works. They refuse to accept either the ruthless debunking of the sceptics or the rather pious idealism of the optimists. The Commonwealth exists and there is no merit in trying to rationalise it or even to justify it. The vast network of committees must be made to work as efficiently as possible.

One particular instance which might perhaps be given is that of the Association of Commonwealth Universities. This is an association of no fewer than two hundred universities. The member states use the Commonwealth Universities Office in London as a recruiting agency for positions within their particular institutions. The vice-chancellors of the universities meet at regular intervals to discuss questions of common interest – such as the development of higher education, the employment of graduates, the role of science in secondary education and a host of other problems of mutual interest and concern. The Commonwealth Universities Association does not exist as a means of propagating any particular ideology, but it certainly does not see itself as a negative, time-wasting or powerless body. It meets its problems as these arise in pragmatic fashion. It has, however, set its face against any participation by the universities in South Africa or Rhodesia in its deliberations.

The Commonwealth will best be understood if the student remembers that it exists because individually its members have calculated that its advantages outweigh its disadvantages. If this suggests a pragmatic interpretation then it is because the Commonwealth carries its members along on an administrative and procedural momentum. The Commonwealth acts as it does because its members are ideologues with regard to procedure but pragmatists with regard to policies. The Prime Ministers meet and survey their problems but formulate no programmes or rigid timetable. The structure is devoid of constitutional law. A previous generation could speak (as did Sir Robert Menzies in 1963) of 'the golden rule of mutual obligation'. This description of the Commonwealth link is clearly over-optimistic. The notion that the Commonwealth has coherence or a single purpose is clearly a thing of the past; thirty-three nations could not so cohere. We hear only of the Commonwealth's conflicts of interests, national ambivalences and of her deep differences and divergences. These manifold cleavages are the end product of the devolution of government from Downing Street to the nationalist successor in a local Government House.

Appendix E (p.154) contains some additional views of the Empire.

2 Empire into Commonwealth

Here's to Queen Victoria
Dressed in all her regalia
With one foot in Canada
And the other in Australia.
Anon.[1]

Politically the British Empire is a clumsy collection of strange accidents. It is a thing as little to be proud of as the outline of a flint or the shape of a potato.
H. G. Wells[2]

In 1897 a *Colonial* conference was held in London; in 1921 an *Imperial* conference was held in London; in 1971 a *Commonwealth* conference was held in Singapore. Whereas in 1897 the British Empire was at its brilliant height during the year of Queen Victoria's Diamond Jubilee, in 1971 the British Prime Minister journeyed to Singapore to spend a large portion of his time in a defence of British policy in residual areas like Rhodesia for which Britain was still nominally responsible. The point may be further illustrated by recalling that in 1914 King George V declared war for all the *colonies* while in 1939, the *dominions* (or independent portions of Empire) decided for themselves whether or not they were at war with Germany. By the late 1940s parts of the Commonwealth were actually fighting against each other.

In 1897 the defence of the Empire was largely the task of the Royal Navy, although the paramountcy of Britain in naval strength was soon to be challenged by the United States and the German Empire. The great prize within the British Empire was of course India, but the Raj was largely symbolic, because its profitability was highly questionable, absorbing, according to modern research, much more effort than it produced in return.[3]

At that time Britain ruled most of her dependencies according to the principle of a simple division between metropolitan sovereign power and its subordinate parts. Indeed John Stuart Mill's lengthy definition of a dependency well described the status of the Empire at the turn of the century. For Mill, dependencies are 'outlying territories of some size and population, which are subject more or less to acts of sovereign power on the part of the paramount country, without being equally represented (if represented at all) in its legislature'. Moreover, at the time of Queen Victoria's Diamond Jubilee the Empire had not yet ceased to grow. Between 1870 and 1898 Britain added about 47 million square miles with a population of 88 million to its Empire. The Britain of 1900 was at the height of its powers. The sun never set on the Empire of 13 million square miles and 360 million inhabitants. India represented about 78 per cent of the population and 14 per cent of the land mass of the British Empire at that time. However, the so-called 'white' colonies were content to live and die British. The most important nationalism in the Empire of seventy-five years ago was British nationalism. The 'ideology' of the Empire, however was imperialism, and to this we now turn.

Imperialism has been defined by Professor Boulding as 'a special case of expansionism in which a political organisation goes beyond the boundaries of its existing society and absorbs heterogeneous peoples and cultures'. Expansionism is a common phenomenon, including the tendency of any social system to expand its structures, and thus includes churches and universities as well as empires. The question is, how systematic was British imperialism? While Britain possessed an empire and as late as 1921, the British 'were not an imperially minded people', they lacked both a theory of empire and the will to engender and implement one'.[4] In short, while the British Empire was a fact, British imperialism was never a philosophy. Many writers, including the English economist, J. A. Hobson, and the Russian revolutionary Lenin, have constructed theories about it but they have superimposed their theories on imperial practice.

Indeed, we will suggest in due course that the Commonwealth itself has followed the Empire's lead in avoiding any philosophical exposition of its objects, aims and purposes. Moreover, if the Secretariat is excluded, the Commonwealth has not even concerned itself with the more humdrum questions of structure, administration or procedure.

The old Colonial Office did of course concern itself with administrative matters, and it 'ran' the colonies for a century or more, functionally, without any real reference to purpose or philosophy. In 1960, however, little remained of the once vast empire, and over 90 per cent of it had been liquidated. The administrative superstructure which had been built up was quietly dismantled and the independent states began their new existences with constitutional expertise provided by British officials.[5]

Imperialism may not then have been a coherent philosophy of empire, but because the British Empire was for long the source of many misconceptions about the true nature of British colonial rule, it may perhaps be worth briefly considering the various notions of empire which have appeared from time to time. Originally, colonial theories were developed in Britain on largely utilitarian lines. Colonial theories prior to the loss of the American colonies in 1776 followed mercantilist lines. Mercantilism – the view that colonies should serve to strengthen the state – developed with the disintegration of medieval unity in Europe. In the absence of any principle for the regulation of interstate affairs, each new nation-state in Europe developed strong antagonistic drives. The need for raw materials, the desire to spread the gospel, the envy of Spain with its massive discoveries of bullion, the belief that England was overpopulated – all these conceptions and misconceptions constituted the rationale for the early Empire.[6] What emerged in due course was an acceptance of the Old Colonial system, which amounted to little more than a system of complete colonial subservience to the supposed interests of the mother country. It was not harshly applied and it was at least an honest system.

Theories of colonial development during the eighteenth century were notable for an almost complete absence of the idea of imperial brotherhood which was so important by the time of Queen Victoria's Jubilee in 1897. There were some exceptions to this proposition amongst whom perhaps the most notable were Lord Chatham and Edmund Burke.[7]

Victoria's assumption of the title Empress of India in 1876 was by no means enthusiastically welcomed by all her subjects.[8] The idea that the British Queen could be regarded as an 'Empress' struck many as distasteful, suggesting as it did some continental, even arbitrary despot. But within a few years, some pride was beginning to be felt in the eminent role (not to mention rule), of the Queen-Empress and the Empire was an object of wonder to many. Towards the end of the century an English economist J. A. Hobson, formulated a theory of 'economic' imperialism. In this theory, imperialism is essentially the product of the desire of investors at home to divert their resources into profitable areas abroad. Hobson's peculiar importance has been well summarised by A. J. P. Taylor, who said of him that he inspired two contradictory tendencies, an explanation of the activities of the English entrepreneurs and an attack upon their motives. Lenin took up Hobson's conclusions and dramatised them. History, Lenin believed, was working against capitalism, particularly in its most developed form of foreign monopoly capitalism. Hobson's argument merely confirmed the whole Marxist thesis regarding the inevitable downfall of capitalism, as well as proving the inherent greed of capitalism.

Imperialism thus became, in the writings of hundreds of polemicists, the great external bogey and the British Empire was represented as its prime manifestation. Every emergent colony took up the theme of imperialism, seeing its troubles as the direct result of British colonisation, conquest and annexation. The theory was stretched to include many Marxist-Leninist variables which could only with difficulty therein be absorbed. The Indian 'outcast' and the African tribal villager were alike portrayed as the 'proletariat', while internal capital formation had to be excluded from the analysis because only 'foreign' capital could be deemed truly to be imperialist. Above all, and at all times, the opponents of the British Empire saw a continuous and systematic conspiracy to keep the colonial peoples in permanent poverty and subjection. For most, indeed, the conspiracy was the whole story. Moreover, it took on racialist overtones as imperialism was directly represented as simple combination between white-rich and black- or brown-poor. In global terms this simpliste interpretation was indeed true; however, in many cases the picture was much more complicated, as is shown in Philip Mason's study *Patterns of Dominance.*[9] In fact British colonial thinking was never consciously racialist, though admittedly it was strenuously paternalist.

The facts suggest that British colonial policy never had a philosophical base, English law has never known legally fixed class divisions, and colonial administrators largely assumed that the better sort of colonials would copy British life and institutions. Victorian imperialism was hardly a 'grand design', let alone a conspiracy, and it lasted essentially for a relatively short period at the end of the nineteenth century and the early years of the twentieth. Lenin's version of imperialism is sheer caricature, particularly as applied to Britain. An 'imperialist' was no more than one who advocated, on a purely technical basis, that economic resources should be diverted to objects within the Empire rather than outside it. Others (like Sir John Seeley) believed that Britain should develop the colonies as a counterweight to the emerging superstates – Russia and America. The most aggressive imperialist was, of course Cecil Rhodes, founder of Rhodesia and Prime Minister of the Cape Colony from July 1890 to January 1896.

Rhodes advocated not a powerful central Empire authority but rather the establishment of semi-autonomous white colonial units bound to the Mother Country through ties of race and blood. The kith and kin argument did not begin with Rhodes, though he gave it added force, meaning and vigour. In many ways he did little more than give powerful expression to what was felt by many statesmen in Australia, New Zealand and Canada.

The 'imperialists' saw the problems of Empire as it were 'from above'. They were mainly concerned with charting the relations between the Mother Country and the outlying parts, seeing the process as a natural and beneficial paternalism. The anti-imperialists looked at the whole problem from a different angle completely. While they naturally resented any attempt to impose a set of policies or institutions upon colonial peoples they nevertheless devoted their energies to assessing the impact of the colonising process upon individuals.[10]

It is important to realise that the British Empire was in essential respects a westernising force which (to use Marx's terms) has 'pitilessly torn asunder the motley feudal ties that bound man to his "natural superiors", and has left remaining no other nexus between man and man than naked self-interest, than callous cash payment'. In this respect the British Empire served merely to give effect to the dynamics which Marx had perceived in bourgeois societies, namely that they should be regarded as essentially progressive forces. Nevertheless while Marx may have been nearer the truth than Lenin, it is much fairer to see the now defunct British Empire as a remarkable human and institutional achievement.

One of the more memorable comments to be made regarding the Empire was by Sir John Seeley, who produced in 1883 the *Expansion of England*, a published version of his Cambridge lectures on the subject.

His observation was that the British Empire was acquired 'in a fit of absence of mind'. Any account of the history of the growth of the British Empire should take account of the fact that it was essentially (with certain exceptions) an unplanned, uncoordinated operation. We might give two examples. In the first place, British people migrated to whichever parts of the Empire they thought might suit them. Between 1815 and 1914 more than 20 million people left the British Isles. Of these about 13 million went to the USA, 4 million to Canada, about 1.5 million to Australia and New Zealand and fewer than 100,000 to South Africa.[11] There was also white settlement in Kenya and in Rhodesia during the twentieth century, but no potential emigrant was ever required to go to a particular territory, with the exception of Australia which for a brief time was a convict colony; but the growth of Australia on this basis alone is very small, and in 1851 Australia's total population was only 400,000.

In the second place we might refer to the evolution of the so-called sterling area. In 1825 Great Britain began to supply her own currency to the colonies; before 1825 they adopted any medium of exchange which happened to be useful, of Spanish, Portuguese, French, Dutch, Sicilian, Indian or other eastern origin. Britain happened to possess the banking facilities to fund many colonial projects. Britain, during the nineteenth century was also the world's leading industrial power, and in 1870 she produced nearly one-third of the world's manufacturing output. The roots of the present sterling area go back over a century, and even though the financial strength of sterling has suffered (partly because of the 'towering stature and bewildering dynamism of the American economy') there is nevertheless a continuing need for a financial framework.[12]

There is therefore little evidence that 'imperialism' conspired to create the Empire in the first place, and none at all to support a conception of the Empire as the unfolding of a great historical plan. It is possible to see in the writings and sayings of Cecil Rhodes a concept of a British destiny to colonise the world for the benefit of the world. It is also possible to quote the poems of Kipling as racialist tracts.[13] Yet while influential for a short period these sentiments were not typical of most observers; most influential students of the Empire (Joseph Chamberlain is an example) merely had a vision of an empire linked together by ties of trade and vague loyalty to the Queen.

The Two Empires

It is customary to speak of two British Empires. Chronologically they can be divided as the Old Colonial Empire, *c.* 1600-1800, and the New Colonial Empire, *c.* 1800-1945.

The Old Colonial Empire. Compared with the Spanish and Portuguese, English overseas trade was slow to start. The Iberian traders were the first to sail to Africa, India and beyond; they were the first to settle and and colonise the New World; they were the first to develop the arts of navigation. Above all, they attempted to develop a monopoly in the valuable spice trade of the East Indies. Spices were the great prize of commerce, required in the European winter as a means of preserving meat and a valuable exchange commodity. It was not until 1580 that Sir Francis Drake reached the Spice Islands.

The Dutch too were rivals and succeeded in creating a monopoly in the East Indies after 1621. The rebuff offered by the Dutch induced British traders to turn to the Indian subcontinent. In the long run, trade with India, started after 1603, was to prove more beneficial than trade with the Spice Islands, and the East India Company, founded under Charter in 1601, steadily built up its factories at places such as the Coromandel coast. Bombay was acquired as part of the dowry of Catherine of Braganza, the wife of Charles II, in 1668. The long history of British involvement in India gradually took shape as more entrepreneurs were attracted by the large profits to be made – normally an average annual dividend reached 25 per cent.

In the New World, unlike India, a good deal of migration from England built up during the seventeenth century. There were two principal waves of colonisation; the first was directed to Virginia, Maryland, the West Indies and South America. The second wave was directed to what were to become the Puritan states of New England. In the first the objective was profit – tobacco, timber, possibly even gold and silver, but in the second, the objective was settlement. The early religious colonists found the process of settlement difficult, and in the first terrible winter fifty per cent of them died.

Settlement of whatever sort was subject to royal decree, grant or charter; thus while Virginia was early developed under a chartered company, Maryland was a proprietory colony whose owner was appointed Governor. The early colonies were permitted to develop elected assemblies. Yet it would be incorrect to envisage the North

American colonies (or more accurately plantations) as nurseries of democracy. In many cases they were unyielding theocracies. The keynote of the Puritan states of New England was religious conformity as the basis of political life. Dissent involved the loss of civic rights: 'a close and intolerant oligarchy utterly untouched by democratic ideals', as one historian described the intolerant Massachusetts.[14]

Another theatre of operations in this phase of imperial development was the Caribbean, particularly Barbados, Bermuda, the Bahamas and Jamaica. These were waters in which British sailors, often no more than pirates, clashed with Spanish and Portuguese, and in another fashion with the Dutch. It was difficult for Englishmen to settle in the tropical and unhealthy Caribbean, yet Barbados flourished on the production of sugar and was then known as 'the brightest jewel in His Majesty's Crown'. The beginnings of the slave trade is largely attributable to the insatiable demand for labour in the sugar plantations. From these inauspicious beginnings the subsequent history of North America took ominous shape. Mercantilism became slowly discredited by 1800, and the creation of the new United States of America meant the loss of five-sixths of the white men in the British Empire.

The loss of the American colonies in 1776 is often taken to be the end of the Old Colonial Empire. Perhaps the protective devices by which the competing European nations attempted to thwart rivals, such as Navigation Acts restricting cargo to British ships, produced a grave weakness. When the American colonies did rebel in 1776, Britain had no ally to support her in her struggle. The other European nations had remained rivals and now took their opportunity to attack the British Empire.

It would be wrong to see Britain, or indeed any European nation, as always consistent in its thinking regarding the Empire. Professor Parry, for example, has discovered traces of ideas of self-determination in very early times: 'The idea, so prominent in present-day theories of colonisation, that subject races should be trained to govern themselves in European fashion, has never been entirely absent from European thought.'[15] Yet this notion was hardly developed in the eighteenth century, and was little understood until the twentieth. However, the old Empire did see further developments in British colonial government which were to lead to important consequences. The first was the Declaratory Acts of 1719 and 1766 which asserted the supremacy of the British Parliament. The imperial Parliament in fact went so far as to abolish the constitution of Massachusetts in 1774, and in the same year passed the Quebec Act which gave constitutional shape to Canada. The second development was the establishment of a Secretaryship of State for the Colonies, an action which foreshadowed the setting up of the colonial department of twenty years later.[16]

The New Colonial Empire. The American War did not bring the Empire to an end. It was indeed reconstituted in those areas which had not been involved in, or had resisted the impulses to, independence which had led to Washington's unilateral secession in 1776. In 1784 the India Act was passed, bringing to an end the irresponsibility of the government of India. Thus control by the home government (or Colonial Office government) was made a counter-balance to the power concentrated in the hands of the local governor or local executive. The Canada Constitutional Act accepted Canada as two provinces and created two advisory bodies, a legislative and an executive council. The question of non-British (i.e. French) colonists was tackled by granting the rights of Englishmen to those living in territories under British sovereignty.

Gradually these early conceptions spread to other parts of the Empire during the nineteenth century, while constitutional machinery was devised which made the administration of the new Empire a more endurable proposition. In particular, thought was given to the creation of an effective central department of state devoted to colonial matters. Between 1801 and 1850 the Colonial Office (as it came to be known) began to take shape, particularly under the directorship of James Stephen (1836-47), the virtual creator of the Crown Colony system. The formation of a Colonial Service to provide the administrators for the growing number of colonies dates from this time. The Colonial Service became unified under the powerful influence of the Indian Civil Service during the Secretaryship of Joseph Chamberlain at the end of the nineteenth century.

Two principal developments may be seen according to whether the territory was 'settled' by British people or whether British officials, soldiers and missionaries administered non-British subject races, though at times the distinction may be blurred. In those territories which were largely colonised by British migrants the question of the most appropriate political institutions was easily resolved: they were expected to operate institutions familiar to Englishmen. The point has been well put by Sir Ernest Barker:

> The fundamental ideas of the Commonwealth are rooted and grounded in principles of English law. . . . It is one of those principles that any man born in the allegiance of the King carries that allegiance with him wherever he may go. . . . If Englishmen could not settle abroad without carrying the King, neither could they settle without carrying a Parliament and the right to assemble and vote taxes in that Parliament. . . . Settlers from other countries (Spain, for example, or Portugal) might carry their King with them. The peculiar thing about settlers from England was that they also carried a Parliament with them.[17]

Before 1832 only one person in twenty of the adult population of Britain enjoyed the vote, and in any case the work which a parliament would be required to do in a distant colony was both meagre and of low repute. During the century which followed, British colonial Acts strengthened the councils and parliaments in those territories deemed appropriate, beginning with Canada (after the Durham Report of 1839, which established the first colonial responsible government) and later extending to South Africa, Australia and New Zealand towards the end of the century. The development of British political institutions such as parliament, cabinet and the party system proceeded naturally and inevitably in the Old Commonwealth.

Difficulties arose, however, where parliaments were looked on as the particular preserve of the white man in racially mixed societies, and where the white settler was forced to share his political institutions either with indigenous people or perhaps migrant workers imported from other races or continents. Hence the British settler is likely to approve of parliamentary government, but not necessarily of election to this parliament on the basis of universal suffrage. The classic example of this situation is in Southern Africa, and more particularly in Rhodesia, where Rhodes' dictum, 'Equal rights for all civilised men' allows a large question mark regarding the question of the interpretation of 'civilisation'.

Canada, Australia, New Zealand and South Africa have all gradually followed the sequence of representative and subsequently responsible government, modified in each case to suit local conditions. A constitutional landmark was reached with the passing of the Colonial Laws

Validity Act, 1865. This act stated, in lawyer's language, that

> No colonial law shall be or be deemed to have been void or inoperative on the ground of repugnancy to the Law of England, unless the same shall be repugnant to the provision of some such Act of Parliament, order or regulation as aforesaid.

In more ordinary language the intention was to permit colonial law-making bodies to make laws for the various colonies without any interference by the British Parliament. In the event of an unlikely clash between these two laws, then the legislation of the British Parliament would be superior. The Colonial Laws Validity Act remained as the centre-piece of Empire relations until 1931.

On the other hand, where a territory was ruled by the British as foreign intruders, a somewhat different situation obtained. British colonial officials usually built on forms of political institutions already developed inside the 'colony' before the arrival of the colonial power. One authoritative definition suggested the following: 'The essence of this system is that traditional rulers and councils are recognised by the colonial government as agents for certain purposes, and given limited authority in a number of fields.'[18] The practice of government by indigenous or local institutions is generally called 'indirect rule'. It was a sop to local leaders, it was likely to be understood by local people, and it was cheap.

Indirect rule began in India, Burma and Ceylon and later spread to Africa, where it became more fully developed by Lord Lugard who described it in his famous book *The Dual Mandate,* written as late as 1922. Lugard's belief, after a long career as a colonial civil servant was that

> Institutions as methods, in order to command success and promote the happiness and welfare of the people, must be deep-rooted in their traditions and prejudices. . . . A slavish adherence to any particular type [of administration] however successful it may have proved elsewhere, may, if unadapted to local environment, be as ill-suited and foreign to its conceptions as direct British rule would be.[19]

The major defect with indirect rule was that it was often built on shaky foundations. While it is true that some African colonies had tribal chiefs who could be seen as local leaders, others did not, and the British appointed chiefs who were never, traditionally, rulers of the people. Moreover, the various nationalists regarded the essentially limited area of local jurisdiction as the attempt of the colonial power to fob them off with the shadow as distinct from the substance of power. In the end most of the later colonies were also given parliamentary forms of government, thus bringing them into line with the old British colonies.

Dominion status and the new Commonwealth

By the end of the nineteenth century, Britain controlled the destinies of many dependencies. In Australia, New Zealand, Canada and South Africa, the conception of dependent status became increasingly inappropriate, particularly as these countries had by 1900 enjoyed internal self-government for periods up to half a century. The notion of being a 'dependency' had certain implied connotations of political subservience or even of immaturity. After the First World War, and given the enormous assistance rendered to Britain by Australia, New Zealand, Canada and South Africa, not to mention others like India for example, it was clear that some new formula was required to denote their status. A conference was held in London to discuss the matter. The term 'kingdom' was felt to be inappropriate when applied to Canada because of its close historical connections with France and the USA.

The new formula selected was that of 'dominion status', which had first been used in connection with Canada, and appears in section 3 of the British North America Act of 1867. After 1907 it was applied to New Zealand officially as an example of a self-governing colony which attended imperial conferences. The term was not used in a pejorative sense of foreign control and quickly became accepted as a technical expression. The United Kingdom and the Dominions were described as

> autonomous communities within the British Empire equal in status, in no way subordinate one to another in any respect of their domestic or external affairs, though united by a common allegiance to the Crown, and freely associated as members of the British Commonwealth of Nations.[20]

This definition has been described as 'the Declaration that Slew the Extinct Dragon', signifying that the old British imperial power to make and break her old Commonwealth was no more. In 1931 the Statute of Westminster was passed to give effect to the resolutions passed by the Imperial Conferences of 1926 and 1930.[21] The Colonial Laws Validity

Act was no longer applicable to the Dominions and the British Parliament terminated its powers to make laws for any Dominion except by mutual agreement. From 1926 to 1931 we can discern a constitutional plateau, as the British Empire quietly gave way to the British Commonwealth of Nations. The term 'British Commonwealth' totally replaced the term 'British Empire' in official usage. By 1948 even the term 'British' had been dropped from normal usage, and the term 'Dominion' was considered inappropriate because it suggested degrees or levels of Commonwealth membership. By 1948 new formulae were required to take care of the arrival of non-British republics within the Empire.

The period of the early 1930s also saw a significant development in the field of imperial economic affairs with the establishment of imperial preferences. Dominion leaders, spurred on by Dominion farmers, argued that the traditional British policy of allowing free entry for, say, Argentine beef and Danish bacon should be replaced by a policy which gave preferences to the Commonwealth rather than to the 'foreigner'. The foreigner should be penalised, so it was felt, by having to pay extra tariffs on his exports. The debate on this matter was almost half a century old by 1930.

At an Imperial Economic Conference held at Ottawa in 1932 there was demonstrated an 'underlying conception of an empire closing its ranks against the outside world'.[22] What this meant was that the spokesmen for various economic interests, from Natal sugar producers to Irish linen manufacturers, attempted to arrange the best bargains for themselves, and this meant excluding the foreigners – the lowest common denominator on which all were agreed. As world trade did not rise at the time the benefits were materially slight, with only a small shift in trade involved. Later the Ottawa agreements proved to be a major difficulty in the negotiations leading to Britain's entry into the European Economic Community in the 1960s. By 1945 the fate of the second colonial Empire was sealed on account of developments partly from within and partly from without. From within pressures mounted for independence as colonial nationalists became more aware of their voice and power, while without, a campaign to terminate colonial rule was conducted by a number of nations indefatigably led by the United States. The second colonial Empire went inexorably into liquidation.

It has been said that while war builds up empires, it also helps to dissolve them. The impact of the Second World War on the Commonwealth was immense. The First World War made direct use of the

Empire's resources. In consequence, great constitutional changes were stimulated in the year after the war. By 1939 it was possible to describe in one phrase the component parts of the whole Commonwealth structure, namely the Commonwealth and Empire. The Commonwealth was commonly taken to refer to the free association of equal and sovereign nations while the Empire referred to the 'subject' races of the more recent colonies.

While it was possible to see the coming and inevitable liquidation of the newer colonies, it was not so easy to visualise the sort of role they would play alongside the older Dominions. Three difficulties faced the Commonwealth in refashioning its constitutional structure in 1947:

1 The new territories wished to enjoy all the privileges of dominion status but were opposed to the ultimate, even if nominal, powers of the monarch. A difficult problem regarding the position of the monarch among potentially republican states arose in 1947, and was settled by the use of an ingenious formula representing the Queen as 'Head of the Commonwealth'.
2 On the whole the peoples of these new territories did not come from British stock and it was felt that their presence would change the whole character of the new Commonwealth. For example, the old terminology would have to be changed. The word 'Dominion', which did not imply 'subjection' under the old dispensation, was, after 1947, unacceptable.
3 As the Commonwealth grew in size it became clear that the old informality would be subject to considerable strain. Decisions could no longer be taken in the almost casual manner typical of the old Dominion Prime Ministers Conferences. A new range of issues faced the Commonwealth concerning the relationship with Britain in its new non-colonial role.

Many informed observers doubted whether the colonies could achieve genuine self-government based on representative parliamentary institutions before the year 2000; others even more pessimistically doubted the wisdom of entrusting the panoply of power in a modern state to peoples who as recently as 1900 were ignorant even of the wheel. The new Commonwealth looked impossible to anybody seeking logic or clarity in international affairs.'The whole system', L. S. Amery had said, 'with its haphazard complexity and lack of coordination on any structural basis, would, I fancy, not be tolerated for a moment by our more logical neighbours across the Channel.'

So far as the old Commonwealth was concerned, the Crown stood out as the 'key mechanism and master symbol of the common history of its members'. All legal and political actions flow from the Crown, including the work of parliaments, judges, soldiers, acts of state. In renouncing the Crown a young republic would appear to be renouncing its rights to remain in the Commonwealth. India, under Jawaharlal Nehru would not accept any restriction on India's rights to republican status. Eventually a solution was found. The preamble to the Statute of Westminster contained this sentence: 'The Crown is the symbol of the free association of the members of the British Commonwealth of Nations.' Hence it was argued that a republican president could co-exist with the British monarch within the Commonwealth. Allegiance to the British monarch was not necessary. The situation 'left entirely intact the monarchical position in Britain and in the countries which wished to retain monarchical institutions; it gave the King a continued status as a Commonwealth institution; it freed India from 'the Crown, with all its associations of coercion and control; and it provided the perfect formula for saving face in Britain and in India'.[23]

A related problem is contained in the notion of Dominion status. The last states to be termed 'Dominions' were India and Pakistan in 1947; by 1950 the term was obsolete. Dominion status did assume the continued supremacy of the monarchy and so was unacceptable. The dropping of the term is highly indicative of the way in which the Commonwealth has striven to discover formulae which both correspond to reality and remain flexible at the same time. More particular reasons for objecting to the continued usage of the term 'Dominion status' are as follows:

1 The term suggested domination by Britain;
2 was not applied to Britain herself and hence suggested that Britain was somehow superior to the other Dominions;
3 was ambiguous and had lost any precision which it had when first used in 1907;
4 did not cover Ireland which has remained a constant constitutional problem;
5 clearly implied a mother – daughter relationship which was no longer appropriate.

Instead of 'Dominion' there emerged the more flexible term 'member of the Commonwealth'. 'Colony' had been rejected for 'Dominion' and this was in turn repudiated to make way for the description which most clearly suggests equality (albeit with some vagueness), namely 'Member of the Commonwealth'. In 1949 the conception of republics within the Commonwealth was novel and untried; in that year there were only eight members of the Commonwealth; by 1969 the Commonwealth had grown to twenty-eight members, with the majority of them republics. The monarch is Head of the Commonwealth and as such holds a special role, whatever the principle of 'equality' might say. Hence in 1957 when the Queen visited the USA and Canada, she visited Canada as Queen of Canada, subsequently visiting the United Nations as Head of the Commonwealth, and later the USA as Queen of the United Kingdom. As if to show the historical relevance of the British connection in the same year, she visited Williamsburg as part of the three hundred and fiftieth anniversary of the foundation of Virginia, the first British Colony in North America. Virginia was settled nearly two hundred years before the formation of the USA and three hundred years before the emergence of the Commonwealth. Gladstone once said that the monarch has exchanged power for influence. It might be more accurate to say that she has further exchanged influence for eminence, and the Commonwealth is likely to have need of this attribute for some time to come.

Current problems

Since 1947 the Commonwealth has had an eventful history. A number of particular problems are of continuing concern.

The American Secretary of State, Dean Acheson made the comment which has now become notorious that 'Britain has lost an Empire but has not found a role'. This remark caused considerable anger in Britain; however, the remark is itself fundamentally unenlightening because even when Britain did have an empire she did not have any precise conception of a role. The practical tasks of serving as the world's policeman or bringer of religion, law and technology to the Empire were never coordinated. While it is true that the colonial Empire posed immense administrative problems, there were never any 'political' (i.e. controversial) problems between its members. The colonies were expected to be 'loyal'.

Since independence has come to the vast mass of the former Empire, certain problems have developed which Britain has been ill-equipped to handle. The Commonwealth has, in like manner as the old Empire, come into being in a fit of absence of mind. Professor Miller says that the Commonwealth grew up 'through inattention'. Some of these problems stem directly from the racial composition of the Commonwealth; the vast majority of its members are not of British ancestry. It was vaguely assumed that after independence, migration between the various parts of the Commonwealth would act according to a self-correcting mechanism. Thus, Indians would stay in India and Chinese in Hong Kong. Englishmen would move to Australia, of course, because Australia's encouragement of immigration from England was official government policy. Yet the lack of any carefully worked out plans regarding Commonwealth migration before 1958 produced a set of laws in hurried response to unexpected shifts in migration. Moreover, the granting of independence to territories like Uganda in 1964 left the question of the rights of the Asian minority in some doubt. While they were allowed to choose British citizenship if they so desired, nobody faced the issue of what would happen if they all came to Britain at one time, as happened in 1972.

Britain's drift into difficulties with Commonwealth members was not always all of her own making. The case of Rhodesia which declared unilateral independence in 1965 is indicative of the new situation, as was Britain's quarrel with Uganda's President Amin in 1972. The fact that Britain was not able to do anything in the physical sense to prevent or end the rebellion in Rhodesia is an illustration of her changed role in the world. The inability to realise this fact led to the gibe that Britain was according to one member of the Commonwealth, a 'humbled toothless bulldog', as if Britain's apparent inability to act was made by choice. Again, when conflicts developed between India and Pakistan, Britain was not really involved (apart from donating £8 million in relief) because in part she had neither the power nor the will to act. The effects on the Commonwealth were, moreover, far reaching. Britain recognised Bangladesh (the new name for East Pakistan) on 4 February, 1972. This recognition came after recognition by the Soviet Union, at the same time as by West Germany and just slightly in advance of the recognition accorded to the new state by the other members of the European Community, with whom Britain had been coordinating her policies on the matter. The Pakistan Government then announced that it would cease to be a member of the Commonwealth and its place was taken by Bangladesh in 1972.

What these actions suggest is that Britain tends to wait on events within the Commonwealth. She is neither a wheel nor a driving force. Whereas the Empire could be run (i.e. administered) in accordance with a set procedure emanating from Whitehall, the new Commonwealth is continually beset by intractable problems of a 'political' nature. This was first dramatically brought out when South Africa left the Commonwealth in 1961. There is no particular way in which Britain can assist in 'healing and settling', for she is not equipped to act as mediator and moderator, for example in India, a subcontinent which she once ruled. Hence some members, sensing the drift of events, have tended to seek the support of non-Commonwealth powers, and to make separate alliances. Canada has for long had a reluctant special relationship with the United States, India has a treaty of friendship with the Soviet Union and Pakistan has an 'understanding' with China, which was perhaps influential in inducing Pakistan to leave the Commonwealth.

Most of the new countries in the Commonwealth are poor and some are amongst the poorest in the world. On average during each year an inhabitant of a state like Malawi will earn US$66, one in Tanzania will earn US$70, an Indian, US$115, and a Gambian will earn US$100. The prospects for decreasing such poverty by greater injections of aid are slight, even if there were no problems to be faced in providing development assistance. Britain's official contribution of about US$500 million per annum represents nearly 0.5 per cent of her gross national product. If private forms of overseas aid are also included, Britain provides about 0.7 per cent of her GNP in total. Most of this assistance is directed towards the Commonwealth, and while the sum provided falls short of the desired one per cent of GNP, it is a better result than is achieved, proportionately by many other developed states.

Yet the provision of aid in itself, without thought as to its proper disbursement, is unlikely to affect basic poverty. In the nineteenth century Britain invested capital in those areas which appeared most likely to produce practical returns, such as railways, docks, harbours and industrial plant. Today, on the other hand, the scope and nature of investment is solemnly debated by economists who argue the merits of investing in unsophisticated preliterate societies and, with the help of sociologists, debate such propositions as 'that the institutional resistances of traditional society is inversely proportional to the size and efficiency of modern inputs'.[24] It is perhaps simpler to remember that the underdeveloped societies will not always respond to the narrow stimulus of economics alone. There are many other obstacles to the development of simple societies, in particular customs, practices, policies, political patronage, administrative capacities, and sometimes in a tenaciously maintained religion. The sacred cows of India remain sacred. India's development therefore awaits a change of heart, or events which are not yet discernible.

While it would be defeatist to argue that the poor areas of the Commonwealth will always be poor, or that the Commonwealth will naturally fall into two categories, rich and white and poor and non-white, it is not easy to see how the two Commonwealths can be reconciled. For example, Canada's per capita GNP figure of nearly $4,700 (1972) contrasts with that found in India where it was no more than $115 in the same year.

The presentday Commonwealth touches many other regional and international associations at many points. The thirty-three member states are all also members of the United Nations, some are members of military pacts such as NATO and SEATO, and some have a particularly strong attachment to particular religious affiliations as was the case of Pakistan and Malaysia in relation to Islam. In a sense, however, the decline of British imperial power has been accompanied by a gradual takeover of old British responsibilities by the USA. It is the leadership of the English-speaking world which matters more and more and this has passed to Washington (though the picture is clouded by the fact that the USA is in a sense also in a period of decline rather than of advance in its position as a world power). Yet compared with the tightly knit post-colonial links of France with her former colonies, the leadership of the English-speaking Commonwealth is open. However, the Commonwealth is not a linguistic union any more than it is a strict political association. The entry of Britain into the EEC has been decisive in demonstrating the new truth about the Commonwealth, that its fundamental problem is one of leadership.

The proposal to join the EEC was first made in 1961, when Harold Macmillan, then Prime Minister, announced his intention to seek Britain's entry. Britain's position at that time appeared to be ambiguous because she sought to combine her proposed membership of the EEC with her primary role as founder of the Commonwealth.

In January 1963 the French President, General Charles de Gaulle, vetoed British membership by the simple expedient of withholding French agreement. In his speech he explicitly turned to Britain's maritime past, specifying 'yet it is true, England is insular, maritime, she is linked through her exchanges, her markets, her supply lines to the most diverse and often the most distant countries'. This was no doubt an answer to Churchill's famous wartime remark that if he had 'to choose between Europe and the open sea, we shall always choose the open sea'. De Gaulle threw back Churchill's taunt in the most effective way, by denying Britain's European letters of credit on the grounds that they were inadequate, suggesting that the Commonwealth was the cause of her ineligibility.

For the next ten years the economic, political, social and cultural arguments were debated in detail, in private and in public. There were few impartial and detached assessments and most people either approved or disapproved. This includes the many economists who produced a welter of facts and figures in an attempt to prove one side of the case or other, but the greatest revelation of all came in September 1971 when fifty-two academic economists wrote to *The Times* stating their view that as far as Britain was concerned the advantages of Common Market membership exceeded the disadvantages. *The Times* printed another letter in which an almost identical number of academic economists stated their view that the economic disadvantages of membership outweighed the advantages. In a sense this correspondence demonstrated something about the whole debate on Europe. The suggestion was that most people decided whether they approved or disapproved of British membership of the EEC in advance and subsequently searched for arguments to justify their stand.

While the debate continued the individual members of the Commonwealth could do little except attempt to negotiate whatever safeguards were possible for each individual member. The individual states hoped that British support would be forthcoming, but in the absence of a firm EEC commitment they could only hope that Britain would speak up on their behalf during the negotiations. There were problems which related specifically to the Commonwealth.

1 New Zealand dairy produce, being temperate, posed a particular difficulty. However, Britain agreed to purchase guaranteed quantities of butter and cheese from New Zealand during the period 1973 to 1977 inclusive, which would mean that in terms of milk equivalent

New Zealand would be selling at least 71 per cent of the 1972 quantity in 1977. Other 'difficult' products such as sugar would be dependent on the goodwill of the EEC sugar beet producers after 1974. Britain consumes about 50,000 tons of sugar per week.

2 Certain areas like Hong Kong were given very limited help. A separate (but not wholly effective) agreement was made giving Hong Kong some generalised preferences under the EEC arrangements. The dependent territories generally were offered association with the enlarged Community with effect from 1 February, 1975.

Those countries within the Commonwealth which had enjoyed a privileged trading position with Great Britain were no longer to be automatically entitled to see the 'mother country' as an automatic market for goods and people. The important point to grasp is simple. The Commonwealth countries had, since 1932, given trading preferences to each other. These preferences would have to be removed if Britain entered the EEC. In place of Commonwealth preferences, Britain would have to accept the Community's common external tariff. The only solution for the Commonwealth was to sell its goods elsewhere. Australia and New Zealand, for example, would have to look more to Asian markets; Canada would have to reappraise its already difficult relationship with the United States; and South Africa, though not a Commonwealth country, would lose her continued preferential position in British markets. The countries whose products could be generally described as 'tropical', and therefore less likely to compete with temperate area European products, were allowed certain rights of entry. There were also less weighty problems, and at one early stage in the negotiations there developed an impasse over the unlikely question of whether Australian kangaroos could be turned into meat and put into tins.

The terms eventually agreed were seen by the Conservative Government in Great Britain as the best which were negotiable – a view which was rejected by some of the leaders of the Labour Party. The question of Commonwealth safeguards became strongly contentious within the Labour Party itself during 1972. Clearly it was a matter of interpretation whether the Labour Government would have accepted these terms while in office. In 1967, Harold Wilson had declared that he 'would not take "no" for an answer' to the question of British membership of the EEC. In 1972 he found himself in open disagreement with his principal lieutenant, Roy Jenkins, who saw the terms offered by the EEC as broadly compatible with Commonwealth needs. There were certain trade union members of the Labour Party who opposed British membership *on principle,* but Mr Wilson was not one of these.

The reaction of the Commonwealth to Britain's proposed membership was generally and naturally unfriendly. When Harold Macmillan announced his intention to seek entry in 1961, the Ghanaian President Dr Nkrumah declared that the object of the EEC was to turn African states into 'hewers of wood and drawers of water', and he saw it as a resurgence of colonialism. New Zealand politicians were alarmed at the prospect of losing their traditional market.

The independent developing Commonwealth countries, excepting those in Asia, were given the choice of three alternatives:

1 Association on the basis of the Yaoundé Convention, which allowed eighteen former French African states to be associated with the EEC;
2 some form of association with the European Community under article 238 of the Treaty of Rome;
3 a looser arrangement, short of association, which would allow them to develop their trade with the enlarged Community.*

Many countries in the Commonwealth felt that Britain's adherence was irrevocable. British intentions were now clearly expressed and whatever Mr Wilson's later view, it is a fact that he too entered an application in 1967. In short, both parties, Conservatives and Labour, accepted the general principle of entry into the European Community. The Commonwealth countries most affected would have to act accordingly and hope that Britain would extract the best possible terms for them. The use of transitional arrangements to allow Commonwealth countries time to adjust became the primary device to cushion the blow.

One important element which has emerged in this discussion has tended to be ignored. British membership of the EEC may be seen as a *psychological* threat to the Commonwealth. The Commonwealth countries appeared to be saying something to the effect that 'we are *hurt* that economic threats should have been made against us by the founder member of the Commonwealth'. Indeed both the economic

* In February 1975, a new convention to replace Yaoundé was signed by 55 countries in the Togo capital, Lomé. The agreement allowed for the third alternative, permitting developing countries (British and French for the most part) to have access to the EEC.

and political arguments frequently suggest the psychological. While agreeing that the economic arguments are of some complexity, no one could really estimate the cost of the harm, so the opponents of British entry tended to stress the harm itself. As for the political arguments, they inevitably became confused with the nationalistic. The Commonwealth has no political rules to break, consequently Britain could not be said to have infringed any; but accession to the EEC may be seen to have had the effect of heightening nationalistic feeling, making conscious both the difference as well as the isolation of many members. It now appeared that Britain was prepared to argue that its future might involve a new family relationship. Despite the assurances that this did not involve 'turning her back' on the Commonwealth, the very fact of British application was a psychological blow to traditional Commonwealth links.

Britain's choice then was made in 1961, when Harold Macmillan first applied for entry to the EEC. At that time Duncan Sandys, Secretary of State for Commonwealth Relations said: 'I believe that my European friends will not misunderstand me if I say that if I were forced to make this cruel choice, I would unquestionably choose the Commonwealth. Happily, we are not confronted with this dilemma.' In fact Mr Sandys was wrong because the Commonwealth read into the application an immensely significant psychological lesson, to the effect that Britain's energy would henceforth be directed towards Europe. So far as the Commonwealth was concerned, while the spirit was willing, the flesh was weak.

However, by the end of 1972, one year after Britain's accession to the EEC, the *Economist* argued as follows.

> It was the last gasp of imperial arrogance that thought the economics of the developed Commonwealth needed any looking after. Australia's exports have been doing so well that they have survived two revaluations of the currency within the year; New Zealand's sheep and dairy farmers are making record profits on the back of high world prices.[25]

At the same time the *Economist* argued that, while excepting the case of sugar, 'the loss of the old Commonwealth preference agreements and bilateral arrangements with Britain has generally proved insignificant in trading terms'. By the end of 1974, it seemed inevitable that, as the *Economist* put it (September 28 1974)

> Britain will not be able to reassert its old influence as the leader of the Commonwealth. Imperial preference is now not much more than a folk memory and the proportion of Britain's exports going to the Commonwealth is falling fast – from 21·88 per cent in 1971 to 18·86 per cent in 1972 and then to 16·60 per cent in 1973

Britain which had for so long controlled the sovereignties of so many and had subsequently donated sovereignty to so many, was now preparing to give portions of her own sovereign powers to a European customs union with an unknown political future. Having made the Commonwealth, Britain would do no more.

3 The Old Countries of the Commonwealth

Love of it across the waters
Binding with electric thrill
Binds our distant sons and daughters
Heart to heart with Britain still.
Flag of Britain (Song, c. 1910)

Britain outside Europe would be a sterile, suety,
ill-tempered and negative province without a metropolis..
Michael Howard[1]

The old Commonwealth countries are Canada, Australia, New Zealand and South Africa. The last of these has now left the Commonwealth but has a past and present intimately connected with the other three. In a sense we should speak of the Big Five if both South Africa and Great Britain herself are included. For many British students the new Commonwealth impinges on their existence through a continuing debate over the problem of Commonwealth immigration. This suggests 'coloured immigration', which has become a highly controversial subject in British politics. Until 1962 Britain freely admitted all Commonwealth citizens to residence, which meant that a quarter of the world's population was entitled to settle in the United Kingdom. By 1961, 170,000 immigrants had exercised their rights, and by 1974 something approaching two million new Commonwealth citizens were living in various parts of the country, though the exact number was a matter of lively debate.

There are of course fewer visible difficulties with Australians, New Zealanders and Canadians. The continued rights of entry of members of the old Commonwealth have in practice caused fewer difficulties. They are 'kith and kin' with a shared history and often identical traditions. The massive reluctance to contemplate their proposed exclusion from relatively free entry into the Mother Country was demonstrated by the technical defeat of the Conservative Government late in 1972 when Conservative Members of Parliament refused to support proposals to give preferred entry to Frenchmen, Dutchmen or Germans over Australians, New Zealanders and Canadians. So far as the USA was concerned, Britain could obtain no more than a 'special relationship'. So far as the old Commonwealth was concerned, the situation, as seen by Professor J. D. B. Miller is that 'Britain is a massive and significant element of their whole range of existence.'[2] Britain exported to them law, political systems, economic philosophies, style, custom, dress and sport. The notion of a common citizenship lasted in the narrow legal sense until 1964 but in the deeper emotional sense may always mean more than the new legality of the Treaty of Rome.

Each of the big three will be considered here in turn. Clearly it would be impossible to set out the major problems facing these countries even in the most meagre outline. However, we set ourselves three specific questions in the hope that the reader may pursue these further for himself. These questions relate to Canada, Australia and New Zealand, and South Africa (included for historical reasons).

1 Who are the Canadians, Australians and New Zealanders?
2 What are their special political problems?
3 What are the major prospects for the future?

Canada

Canadians are the senior members of the Commonwealth. Their problems have frequently been solved by reference to principles which have later become the essential constitutional basis of the Commonwealth. In 1776 they remained free loyalists, in 1867 Canadians established the first example of a voluntary union of provinces tied to the British Crown, ultimately producing the first High Commissioner, and it was in Canada that the notion of dominion status was born.

Voltaire casually dismissed Canada with the imperious comment: *quelques arpents de neige* (a few acres of snow). The few acres of snow are in fact close on 4 million square miles of land and fresh water: over forty times the area of Britain. Canada is in some respects the model Dominion, set up as a federal state by the British North America Act, It now consists of ten provinces: Ontario (acceded to federation 1867). Quebec (1867), Nova Scotia (1867), New Brunswick (1867), Manitoba

(1870), British Columbia (1871), Prince Edward Island (1873), Saskatchewan (1905), Alberta (1905), and Newfoundland (1949), Reference must also be made to the Northwest Territories (1870) and the Yukon Territory (1898).

Canada's population consists of rather more than 20 million people, about 9 million of these of British stock and about 7 million French Canadian in origin. Germans, Ukrainians, Italians and Dutch constitute the rest of the population. The 'original' Canadians, Eskimos and Indians today make up about 1.2 per cent of the total population.

There are three basic cleavages which produce divisions in the Canadian nation. These are the questions of English and the French Quebec separatists, Protestant and Catholic antagonism, and relations with Britain. French Canadians constitute a historic bloc of 7 million people who have for long felt themselves to be second class citizens but who have recently won important concessions. Religious antagonisms are less acute, but the delicate balance between Catholic and Protestant ensures subtle religious competition in the cities.

Canada has often been described as a nation in search of itself, engaged on a national search for self-identification. Canadians live in North America but would prefer that others regard them as other than Americans. The Canadian Prime Minister, Pierre Trudeau, visited Washington in March 1969 and said: 'Living next to you is in some ways like sleeping with an elephant. No matter how friendly and even-tempered is the beast, if I may call it that, one is affected by every twitch and grunt.' It has been said that Canada aspires to combine the skills of the British in government, the knowhow of the Americans and the culture of the French. What they sometimes perceive as the Canadian reality is British knowhow, American culture and French government, as one wag expressed it.

Hence for somewhat negative reasons, Canadians still frequently turn to Britain and to the Commonwealth in some part to emphasize their distinctness from a culture to which they are so close. It is unlikely, however, that the ties with Britain can strengthen, particularly when it is remembered that about 45 per cent of the country's 20 million people are under twenty years of age, whereas two decades ago this figure was only 37 per cent. It is of course the older rather than the younger Canadians who feel an attachment to Britain.

Canada's effective constitution is the British North America Act 1867, which defines the relationship between the provinces. A confederation was established called the Dominion of Canada, consisting of Nova Scotia, New Brunswick and Lower and Upper Canada, the last two becoming the provinces of Quebec and Ontario. Today Canada's ten provinces extend from the Atlantic to the Pacific. Canada has a bicameral (two-chamber) form of government, consisting of a Senate (102 senators) and a House of Commons (264 MPs).

The most frequently discussed problem in Canadian politics is that of Quebec nationalism. For decades many English-speaking Canadians have refused to contemplate the problem, which in a sense has always been present if not sufficiently recognised in Canadian politics. Since about 1960 Quebec nationalism has become increasingly militant.[3] Canada's problem is that it has two main ethnic and linguistic groups each too firmly bound to a mother-culture to be able to overwhelm the other. If Quebec does ultimately secede from the federation, English Canada may be swept into the American melting pot.

The perennial problem of the French Canadians and their demand to be recognised as different makes it almost impossible to change the constitution, though a project to revise it is the subject of a long-term federal-provincial study. Commissions have sat for long on the subjects of bilingualism and biculturalism, and in 1969 Canada's House of Commons approved a bill making the French language the equal of English throughout the federal government. The French have not forgotten or forgiven the defeat of Montcalm by Wolfe at Quebec in 1759. An interesting parallel may be drawn between the French Canadians and the descendants of the Dutch, the Boers in South Africa and the English intruders who defeated them (but less effectively) in 1901. The major difference between Canada and South Africa is that French separatism was contained, or at least found no room for development, while Boer separatism developed and triumphed. The French Canadians are in some respects the Afrikaners of Canada, without the vital African element beneath.

Canada has other potential forms of separatism. Given the enormous size of the country, almost 6,000 miles from east to west, the interests of the prairie and Pacific coast provinces are only barely compatible with those of, say, the Atlantic coast, and frequent pressure for secession emanates from western Canada. British Columbia's interests in no way harmonize with those of Nova Scotia and Newfoundland, and the Canadian federation suffers accordingly. If Quebec is given special treatment and its demand for a separate identity is fully met, then the federal government in Ottawa is likely to receive further demands for special treatment; separatism may be a luxury which a united Canada cannot afford. Hence the question facing any government in power in Ottawa is clear: how far can Quebec's claims be satisfied without unleashing a constitutional crisis which would endanger the whole deliberate balance of the Canadian confederation by encouraging centrifugal forces all over Canada? In these circumstances any institution or force which can help provide cohesion is to be retained and perhaps even cherished.

Canada's problems derive essentially from the federal structure and are basically geographical. There is no fundamental conflict over class, labour or socialism. Neither of the two major parties is socialist or even left-wing by European standards; even the small fabian-type Social Credit party obtained only 7 per cent of the votes in the 1972 election.[4] In Australia and New Zealand the Labour Parties remained in opposition respectively for twenty-three years and twelve years, and both succeeded in their return to office in 1972. In Canada, on the other hand, there was a decided swing to the Conservative Party under Robert Stansfield. In regard to socialism, Canada resembles the United States far more than it resembles Australia, New Zealand and the United Kingdom. The small Social Credit Party has traditionally been stronger in the prairie provinces than in the eastern part of Canada, Quebec excepted, though it suffered reverses in provincial elections in 1972.

For very long periods until the First World War, Canada operated virtually a single-party system. The Liberal party won elections with considerable regularity. Gradually the Conservatives found their strength, and they won the election in 1958. The result is that Canadian federal politics now demonstrates signs that it is a qualified two-party arrangement.

On the assumption that the Canadian confederation is secure, future prospects depend to a large extent on the United States. The Commonwealth is of much less importance. At present Canadian *mores* differ little if at all from those typical in the United States. However, Canadians believe that there are important if rather subtle differences between themselves and the great Republic to the south. In the first place, Canada is subordinate to the military system over which they have little ultimate control; for example, the United States sees Canada as a buffer zone in terms of its anti-Soviet missile defence system. As Canadian territory extends to within five hundred miles of the North Pole, such a conception is perhaps not entirely unexpected. However, Ottawa had no voice in the decision taken by the USA to set up the so-called Safeguard antiballistic missile system, notwithstanding the fact that in any nuclear exchange the colliding missiles would obviously meet over Canada. Set beside this situation the defensive power of the Commonwealth looks very weak indeed.

In the second place, Canada has a large conscience, and regards itself as a society far more humane than its giant neighbour. There is little or no racialism in Canada and, according to white Canadians no tension exists between Canada's 60,000 blacks and white Canadians. At the same time the opportunities accorded to Canada's 250,000 Indians have been considerably less than those accorded to white Canadians. Again, all those young Americans who wished to avoid conscription for Vietnam were welcomed by many Canadians, and after 1969 even actual US army deserters were permitted to seek refuge in Canada. In the Commonwealth itself Canada was always regarded, but particularly after 1968 with the advent of Mr Trudeau to power, as the closest supporter of the interests of the new members of the Commonwealth, consistently finding itself as the Commonwealth's radical spokesman. At home, in 1969, Mr Trudeau piloted a controversial 'morals' bill through the Canadian parliament (making this his first real trial of strength). Canada's criminal code was radically liberalised by a series of new measures on homosexuality, abortion, lotteries, probation and the penal system more generally.

Canada's relations with Britain depend to some degree on the continuance of the monarchical connection. Many older Canadians feel a strong attachment to the monarchy and a survey carried out in 1968 suggested that many young people also favour the continuance of the royal connection, though others regard it as an anachronism. One Canadian department of political science discovered that Queen Elizabeth II had a lineal connection with a medieval Ukrainian prince. In a province like Alberta this discovery is important because there are perhaps a million Ukrainian Canadians residing there.

It would be wrong to assume that Canadians feel attached to Britain merely because some of them feel attached to the monarchy; after all, the Queen *is* Queen of Canada. Nevertheless the likelihood is that the monarchy will gradually disappear in Canada. Quebec's Nationalists wish an immediate Republic, and it may well be that Ottawa may find, in the game of chess that is politics, that Queen has become pawn. There is certainly no comparable tender feeling in Canada regarding the President of the United States.

Canada's continuing problem is therefore the problem of its identity. While they do not wish to belong 'spiritually' to Britain, they resent the fact that Canada is largely a client state or a satellite of the United States. Nearly 70 per cent of the Canadian economy is in the hands of the USA and in some sectors, notably the automobile industry, the figure is 100 per cent. Yet while the economic power over Canada held by the USA is immense, the Americans would not really want Canada's political problems as well as their own. Relations between the two are a constant demonstration of an unhappy situation in which the partners live in sin, having survived flirtation and yet rejected marriage. The outside observer cannot really detect much difference between the *ethos* of Canada and that of the United States. In particular, when Mr Trudeau became Prime Minister in 1968 he 'emerged' from a contest from within the Liberal Party in a typically North American, rather than in a 'British' way. Politics in Canada has become a contest not so much of parties as of personalities. This style of personalised politics has not eluded Britain but it has gone much further locally in Canada. Classical parliamentary democracy is infinitely more difficult to manage from the perspective of Ottawa, 5,000 miles away from British Columbia, than it is from London, only 400 miles away from Edinburgh.

Australia

Australia is a territory as large as Western Europe, surrounded by densely populated Asian neighbours whose peoples are very different culturally and psychologically from Australians. Apart from drawing on her British cultural heritage, Australia has for long been introspective and it is only thirty years since her first diplomatic post outside Great Britain was opened. However, Australia has no powerful neighbour at hand to provide instant defence, as Canada has the United States; hence Britain and Australia must retain some defence links.

The Australians could be described as race-conscious egalitarians. While in contrast with the British, essentially outgoing, unpretentious and 'matey', they are suspicious about non-white Asians, and insensitive towards their Aboriginal citizens. The so-called white Australia policy has officially ceased to exist, but Australians are not yet prepared to accept the implications of unlimited Asian immigration. Australia, it has been said, began as a British gaol, and developed successively as a vast grazing ground, a source of minerals, a granary and a larder, and a highly protected industrial machine. At present wool, beef, wheat, dairy products and minerals account for 85 per cent of exports. Mineral development has been rapid; Australia leads the world in production of lead and zinc, and it is clear that the volume of resources is still largely untapped. However, Australians are basically urban creatures, with 83 per cent of the population living in towns. Sydney and Melbourne account for over 5 million people out of the total Australian population of 12.5 million.

Australia's history has been largely an economic history concerned with the spread of her early pioneers across the massive island continent. Six 'states' have been created and were welded into a Commonwealth (to use Australia's own terminology) in 1901. The six colonial governments surrendered part of their powers to create a new federal structure. During the First World War Australia, with a population of about 5 million all told endured more soldiers killed than the United States whose population was then twenty times as great, and New Zealand suffered proportionately even more casualties. The Australasian territories were expected to be loyal colonies and the war demonstrated this loyalty beyond doubt.

Until recently Australia was regarded by the British in somewhat cavalier fashion as a mere extension of Britain, but huge mineral discoveries, coinciding with a quickening of the pace of life in Australia, have led to a reappraisal of its potential. Predominantly pastoral ways have given way to a rapid era of industrialisation. The changes of the past decade have made Australia into a regional Asian power, a situation summed up in a Japanese newspaper which stated that 'Australia stands on a tripod of Britain, the United States and Japan.'

Australia's brand of nationalism was in process of development during the nineteenth century. What emerged was a mixture of radicalism and national self-assertiveness, possibly a reaction against the closely knit colonial system. From these components twentieth-century Australia has evolved. A particularly strong current of thought believed that Australia could develop a promised land in the southern hemisphere distinct from the values of the Old World and the inequalities of life in Britain.

Australian nationalism is not dissociated from the English-speaking world and its culture; rather it may be best regarded as a feeling that Australia can and does occupy a special place in the English-speaking world. Life and institutions there are essentially urban, in spite of the economic development in terms of sheep and minerals. There has never been a successful movement for total renunciation of the British connection, if one excepts such transient and remote episodes as the riot of discontented gold-miners of 1851 who declared the Republic of the Southern Cross and built the Eureka Stockade at the Ballarat gold-fields. During the twentieth century, Australians have come, naturally, to insist on their separateness and their distinctive culture.

The influx of New Australians, that is of immigrants not from British stock, has had some effect in changing the fundamentally British ethos of the country. Greeks, Italians, Yugoslavs and Poles have little or no attachment to the conventional Australian mother country. Many Australians, strongly influenced by their need to grapple with their huge frontiers, demonstrate an absorption with the pursuit of things material, and it has been cruelly said that they have not yet fully developed 'the art, as distinct from the standard, of living'.[5] The age of Sir Robert Menzies, Prime Minister for sixteen years, has passed. Sir Robert, described as the 'last of the Queen's Men', was at home in a Britain which made him a knight of the Thistle, Privy Councillor, Companion of Honour, Queen's Counsel, Fellow of the Royal Society, Lord Warden of the Cinque Ports and Constable of Dover Castle.

While Sir Robert, like so many Australians was 'British to the boot-straps' his successor was described as 'all the way with L.B.J.', thus reflecting the presumed dilemma facing Australia of not knowing which way to turn. Essentially, as Professor Miller, himself an Australian, suggests:

> The typical Australian picture of Britain became one of a little island tightly packed with humanity, carefully graded into social classes, run by aristocrats with Oxford accents, capable of developing worthy institutions, but also to be deplored for its treatment of the convicts and its heartless retention of the slums. Britain was the land of fog, rain, dirt, factories, slag-heaps, privilege; Australia was the land of sun, blue skies, outdoor living, cleanliness and opportunity.[6]

However, the United States was hardly welcomed unreservedly as a cultural substitute, in spite of the earlier defence arrangements which involved Australia, New Zealand and the United States. The various 'British' sports for example are played with such a tenacity in Australia (and perhaps even more so in New Zealand), that it is difficult to see how the Australian life-style can become permanently subordinated to the lure of the USA.

Australian politics at the federal level has been remarkably stable. From 1949 to 1972 the coalition of Liberal and Country parties held power without effective challenge from the opposition Labour Party. For most of this time the coalition was dominated by the personality of Sir Robert Menzies who 'reigned' from 1949 to 1965 and whose voice came to be synonymous with that of Australia. The official Opposition was the Labour Party at first under Dr H. V. Evatt and then A. A. Calwell. In the mid-1950s the party split and one group formed the Democratic Labour Party. Because of the Australian usage of preferential voting, the Government benefited from the votes cast for the DLP.

After twenty-three years the 'pendulum' swung slowly enough to allow the Labour Party under Gough Whitlam to regain power, but he was forced into an election in mid-1974. Yet Australia is not easily ruled from the centre. The six states ensure that it is a federal state rather than a single political entity. Each state, New South Wales, Victoria, Queensland, South Australia, Western Australia, even the Northern Territories, regards its own government and politics as *sui generis.* The issues facing Australia in the 1970s appear to be as follows.

Relations with Asia in general and China in particular. Throughout the whole postwar tenure of office of the Australian Liberal and Country parties the attitude to Asia, and particularly to Communist Asia, was hostile. After the return of the Labour Party to power in 1972 China was quickly recognised and Australian forces were brought home from Vietnam. A good neighbour policy was adopted. A more flexible, if selective immigration policy was also envisaged, though one doubts whether a White Australia policy can ever be fully discarded. Australians will move slowly in the direction of greater liberalisation of immigration. Asia is an uncertain prospect. China is a communist threat, but Japan is a commercial threat. Australia's problem is that it is *in* Asia but not *of* it.

Relations with Britain. Almost immediately after the victory of the Labour Party in 1972, the designated High Commissioner to London, John Armstrong, stated that Australia would certainly become a republic. In practice this was a rational decision which would in no way alter Australia's rights and role. Many Australians, however, resented the idea, because apart from South Africa's special case, none of the old dominions had ever officially contemplated republicanism.

Internal development. Most people believe that Australia's further economic development is likely to be both intensive and extensive (given the size and resources of the country). The growth of the economy is necessarily dependent on large-scale investment, which, to a large extent is likely to come from the USA together with Japan, and to a smaller extent from Great Britain. Large areas of the Australian economy are under the control of multinational corporations. Over 75 per cent of the motor car industry is controlled by foreigners, while 60 per cent of Australia's considerable mineral production is also outside Australian hands, as well as many other industries. It remains to be seen whether investment and expertise from the United States is likely to increase cultural Americanisation.

The Aborigines. There are about 45,000 pure-blooded representatives of the original Australians and about 80,000 persons of mixed blood (in 1788, the numbers of aborigines was 251,000). The official policy is one of total assimilation. Unofficially, white Australians have sometimes manifested racial attitudes to the Aborigines not far removed from the attitudes of Afrikaners to Africans in South Africa. The Aborigines were given the right to vote in 1962 and were not counted in a census until 1967; some groups have become assimilated in sport (Miss Yvonne Goolagong in tennis) as well as in a very small token fashion in politics (Senator Nicols), but for the most part they have been shuffled off from the large cities and spend most of their lives in poverty and without education, and even without hope.

Australia, like Canada, is a federation and 'the fundamental and distinguishing characteristic of a federal system is that neither the central nor the regional governments are subordinate to each other but are instead co-ordinated'.[7] British students, accustomed to studying Britain as a unitary state, should not forget that the Commonwealth contains many federations, such as Malaysia, Nigeria and India. What the federal system implies is that, while legally Australia is a stronger or truer federation than that found in Canada, the outside negotiator is really dealing with as many as six states in say African terms. The economic and political power of New South Wales or British Columbia, far exceeds that of, say, Malawi or Sierra Leone, who are members of the Commonwealth in their own right.

New Zealand

New Zealand was first visited by Captain James Cook in 1769 but British settlement began only in the nineteenth century. Even after the signing of the Treaty of Waitangi in 1840, Maori wars continued intermittently until about 1870, largely because the Treaty was not regarded seriously by the New Zealand Company. New Zealand's prosperity was to be based on the wool industry. In 1853 this was valued at £67,000 but by 1870 total exports exceeded £4 million. By 1914 New Zealand's foreign trade stood at £45 million, 63 per cent of it being with Great Britain. New Zealand's dependence on Great Britain has been at the centre of her difficulties over British accession to the EEC.

It must always be remembered that New Zealanders are not Australians; their life-style is definitely though subtly different. New Zealand consists of two principal islands, North Island and South Island lying 1,200 miles south-east of Australia, with a population of about 3 million, about 250,000 of whom are Maoris. Most of the present-day inhabitants trace their origins back to the British Isles, particularly to Scotland and much of their way of life retains a Scottish element.

New Zealand's standard of life is high and unemployment is low. A paternalistic social welfare system guarantees a high level of social services. Sociologists have stressed the extraordinary apathetic blandness of New Zealand life, and there is some debate as to whether a high tax rate and guaranteed social security has dulled incentive and ambition. The immigration authorities clearly prefer immigrants to be of British stock though in 1974 unrestricted entry of Britons to New Zealand was stopped, and some people discern a change in the New Zealand national character as non-British immigrants enter the country. Britain's entry into the EEC will also influence New Zealand's view of the 'Old Country' because it is New Zealand more than any other Commonwealth country which is likely to be materially affected. However, contrary to popular view, only 13 per cent of the New Zealand population is fully engaged in agriculture, in comparison with 30 per cent in manufacturing industries and 18 per cent in distributive and financial sectors. New Zealand is therefore not the placid pastoral country of the early years of this century, but is becoming a diversified industrial state possessing rich mineral deposits. There are large steel mills near Auckland and a massive aluminium smelter in the South Island.

New Zealand's relatively straightforward government system was created by the British Parliament's Constitution Act of 1852. It is a unitary system without federal complications. New Zealand was created a 'Dominion' by Order-in-Council in 1907, and was a founding member of the Statute of Westminster club in 1931.

New Zealand developed through a system of group settlement in a way totally dissimilar from Australia which is a good example of uncoordinated colonial development. This happened partly as a result of the efforts of Edward Gibbon Wakefield, who developed the idea of 'systematic colonisation' and who wished to induce a better sense of organisation and development in New Zealand in contrast to Australia, where growth was seen as haphazard and under the control of adventurers.

In November 1972, and after an unbroken period of twelve years in office, the National Party led by John Marshall, was defeated in a general election which returned the Labour Party to power in Labour's biggest win in a New Zealand general election since the party first came to power in 1935. The Labour Party, then led by Norman Kirk (and afterwards by Wallace Rowling) obtained fifty-five seats, as opposed to the National Party's thirty-two seats in the House of Representatives in a total assembly size of eighty-seven. The Labour Party's policy was for higher welfare spending as well as that on regional development and housing, while the National Party appeared to want to develop sound trading policies, particularly with regard to the EEC, as well as greater industrial development at home.

Some people regard the future of New Zealand as unpromising because of its dependence on a Britain which sees its future in Europe. There are in particular two interrelated problems ahead. With a population of about 3 million and a work force of about 1,250,000, the nation is developing faster than its capacity to meet the needs of industry, commerce and social services even though the work force has increased by 22.9 per cent in the last decade. This problem was disguised for some years because New Zealand imported skills from Britain, Australia and Holland. In 1967 the international wool market suffered a recession and the New Zealand dollar was devalued. Instead of being an importer of skills, New Zealand began to experience a loss of qualified persons, particularly doctors and academics as well as technologists. The size of New Zealand implies a reduced scale of opportunities compared with other highly industrialised nations: a really talented New Zealander is likely to have to leave the country if his ambitions are thwarted.

One New Zealand intellectual, Professor Keith Sinclair once asserted that New Zealand would become the 'sleepy hollow of the South Pacific and sink into a life of intellectual torpor' unless a new immigration policy was devised to retain present and encourage new skills. No country wishes to feel that it is experiencing an intelligence decline and white New Zealand is by no means devoid of high-quality talents, but it will have to 'run very fast in order to stay where it is'. Above all, in a country which has depended for so long on British immigration, values and ideals, it is no doubt galling for many New Zealanders to see Britain integrating into a European concert of nations. Nevertheless there are signs that New Zealand may still be very attractive, even to 'European' Britons, as a place of refuge from British economic ills.

South Africa

Although South Africa terminated its association with the Commonwealth in 1961, before that date it was an important Old Dominion and a signatory of the Statute of Westminster in 1931. Indeed South African statesmen such as Smuts and Hertzog were in the forefront of Commonwealth formation and structure and it was they rather than British statesmen who wrestled with definitions of terms such as dominion status. Over a long period South Africa has had close historic ties with Britain, dating back to the Napoleonic wars and including the two anglo-Boer wars which ended in 1901, and today about 40 per cent of the Republic's white population is of English descent. Trading links have been particularly close and although South Africa left the Commonwealth in 1961, Britain still gives certain trading preferences to South Africa which are threatened by Britain's membership of the EEC.

A writer on South African affairs once produced an article entitled, 'There are no South Africans'. It takes little imagination to see why, though such a title might shock South Africans, it is in many respects quite an appropriate description of the South African scene. Those people who live in the Republic of South Africa do not form a compact homogeneous group. There are two quite distinct groups of Whites. First the Afrikaners, who are the descendants of the Dutch or Boers (Boer means farmer), with a strong admixture of French Huguenots and Germans: this group comprises nearly 60 per cent of the white population and effectively controls the policies of the entire Republic. The Republic of South Africa (created from the 1910 Union of South

Africa in 1961) is the Afrikaner's Republic, for Afrikaners dominate in the army, bureaucracy, police and, because of the majority of their Nationalist Party in Parliament, the political system, but much less securely the economy. South Africa presents an interesting example of a cleavage between the economic and political aspects of national development. Afrikaners have firm control over the Civil Service and have shaped South African policy on race issues.

The second group is of the English-speaking South Africans who comprise about 40 per cent of the white population. There has been a remarkable change in the fortunes of the English-speaking section over the past half-century. In 1910 the Union of South Africa was established and reconciliation appeared to have become acceptable to both white groups, suggesting that the bitterness of the war had passed. Indeed the Boers or Afrikaners appeared, through their leaders, two former Boer soldiers, Smuts and Hertzog, to accept their role and that of South Africa as part of the British Empire. The Afrikaners spent the first years of the twentieth century engaged in a struggle for survival to prevent their becoming a class of 'poor whites'. Yet in the 1930s and 1940s it became clear that Afrikaner nationalism (which was incidentally the first form of African nationalism) was strongly supported; in 1948 the Nationalist party came to power and has remained in power ever since. The election of 1948 gave the Nationalists a majority of five seats and they proceeded to create the Afrikaner state in the Southern portion of Africa. The climax of Afrikaner political monolithism was reached in 1960 when, in a republican referendum, a small majority demonstrated its support for the creation of a South African Republic.[8] In 1961 South Africa withdrew from the Commonwealth and the English-speaking group found itself isolated, confused and dependent on the goodwill of their former enemies.[9]

A third group comprises the Coloureds, who are of mixed race, partly African, partly Malay and partly European, numbering approximately 2 million. They normally speak Afrikaans as a first language but are not accepted as true Afrikaners by their white compatriots. The Coloureds are largely restricted to the Cape Province, in and around Cape Town, though there are a considerable number in the Transvaal. The Coloureds fill most of the jobs as artisans, mechanics, shop and factory workers, but they are not permitted to take employment reserved for whites.

The Natal Indians who were brought as indentured labour to work on the sugar plantations on the Natal coast in the late part of the last century, form another minority group. There are restrictions on the movement of Indians throughout South Africa and they have become essentially a Natal problem. South African Indians have prospered in commerce, although the full force of apartheid applies to them as it does to the Black Africans. The South African government has made attempts to have them repatriated to India but the conditions of the repatriation have not been acceptable to either side.

Black Africans make up almost three-quarters of the entire population. It is incorrect, however, to regard them as a single group because they represent many subgroups and tribes. When the first Europeans landed at the Cape in 1652, they found that certain tribes were already inhabiting the huge area of what is now the Cape Province. These were the Bushmen and Hottentots, but the group known as the Bantu (using the word in the strictly anthropological sense) were only at the beginning of a southward migration. As the whites spread into the area of the North Cape and subsequently into newer areas, so the Bantu spread into the same areas in several waves. Today, the South African Bantu Africans can be divided into four main groups: Nguni, consisting of Zulu, Swazi and Xhosa; Sotho who are the Tswana, Pedi and Southern Sotho; The Venda of the Northern Transvaal and the Shangana Tsongo who straddle the Eastern Transvaal and Mozambique. The total number of Black Africans of all groups is about 17 million with about 30 per cent living in 'white' towns and 30 per cent working for white farmers. South Africa's history has in many ways followed a pattern in which white immigration has created towns which have become Africanised, with many consequent social problems. The towns are nominally controlled by whites, who rely on non-white labourers to carry out the multiplicity of tasks required in a complex urban environment.

White South Africa has become associated with a political ideology known by its Afrikaans term 'apartheid'. Apartheid, or apartness, implies racial separation but the term has gained a pejorative sense in that it is generally taken to refer to discrimination by white people against black. It is perhaps useful to distinguish between what is sometimes called 'grand' and 'petty' apartheid. Grand apartheid refers to the proposed division of the political entity of South Africa into smaller but subordinate sovereign units. The proposed policy is called 'separate development' and the areas set aside for black settlement are called bantustans. The area on the eastern Cape called the Transkei is regarded as the first Bantustan; its powers are heavily circumscribed in spite of the fact that it has a black prime minister. Petty apartheid refers to the practice of racial discrimination in towns in shops, on public transport, in government offices, facilities and in all manner of shared resources. The laws of South Africa currently entrench petty apartheid, legislating in a vast area of social life, from schools to sex.

Apologists for apartheid assert that what petty apartheid there is will fade away in due course as Africans move to their 'homelands' or 'bantustans' and leave the white urban areas. Opponents argue that petty apartheid is a reality and that grand apartheid is a fraud or a stratagem to ensure white supremacy for all times. It was over the question of apartheid that South Africa's position within the Commonwealth became intolerable. South Africa's problems may appear to the outsider to be the product of a wilful and barbarous colour policy, yet the internal perspective is different, and this policy has not fundamentally affected the position that the peoples of South Africa co-exist in a mixed economy. There is some truth in the assertion that 'there are no South Africans', and indeed 'South Africa is a geographical, and neither a cultural nor a political expression'.

The political life of South Africa is fundamentally structured on a simple premise. Political power is centralised to a degree through the logic of cabinet concentration. South Africa has a parliamentary system which has been brilliantly manipulated by a party dedicated to the achievement of power in order to create a society of its own desired image and likeness. The system involves two 'operational requirements'. It permits the winner of an election to obtain full political power provided it can win a simple majority of the seats in the parliament; it further assumes that such power will be exercised responsibly and by consultation with minorities. The Nationalist party understood that its accession to power entitled it to everything this accession implied, but did not grant that the second proposition relating to minority rights necessarily followed. In 1952 the Nationalist party used its parliamentary majority to remove from the South African constitution certain entrenched rights. At bottom the ideology of apartheid was to precede parliamentary procedures; parliamentary government was so construed as to exclude its concomitant virtue of 'fair play'.

There are many states, in Commonwealth Africa and outside, in which power has been appropriated and cynically manipulated for selfish purposes. None of these has put this talent to better effect than South Africa. Since 1948 the white South African Parliament has operated in a fashion recognisable to British parliamentarians with a government (National Party) and opposition (United Party), periodical elections and outside, a vigorous political dialogue in a reasonably free press. The South African Nationalist party knows, however, that the chances of its losing power even after twenty-five years are slight, mainly because it has the unswerving support of the Afrikaner majority; but such a possibility is not totally impossible and the pendulum could swing in the other direction. South Africa is not a single party state any more than is Australia or New Zealand, but a change of majority party is likely to be of greater significance in the Republic than in either of the other two. This is not to suggest that the Opposition United Party would effect any change in policies, but in social terms the Afrikaners would be forced to share their currently predominant place in the administration, police and army in a manner to which they are now unaccustomed. A struggle for power would be more likely to develop within South Africa at an intermediate level, not over the larger issues of grand apartheid but more possibly over patronage in government.

Outside or inside the Commonwealth, South Africa is likely to be a bone of contention. Its racial policies have infuriated Black African states in such a way that any continued contact with the Republic by any Commonwealth state is likely to induce bitterness. Britain, for example, has continued to supply arms to South Africa for the purpose of maritime defence and to maintain large investments in the country as well as carry on an extensive trade under preferential conditions. Many thousands of British workers (for example in the port of Southampton) derive a living from the South African connection. It would be very difficult indeed for Britain to cease its trade with South Africa.[10] A country like Tanzania on the other hand, manifests an implacable hostility and provides guerrilla training for the various bands of 'freedom fighters' from South Africa, Rhodesia and the various former Portuguese-controlled territories, Angola and Mozambique.

The Commonwealth will have to live with South Africa on its conscience for some time to come.

The old white Dominions and Great Britain

Until about 1950 the old white Dominions saw themselves as enjoying a relaxed and easy relationship with the Mother Country which, in its turn, could rely upon their loyalty. They saw themselves as members of a free and equal association of member states, each on exactly the same model and taking their cue from the Statute of Westminster. Some even saw a family relationship persisting. A number of points have been suggested in this chapter which we may now further examine by way of summary and conclusion.

Australians, New Zealanders, Canadians and even South Africans and Rhodesians are frequently regarded as British in emotional terms. The 'kith and kin' argument and attachment is still very strong in spite of a gradual drifting away from Britain by the old Dominions. At the end of 1972 the British Government was defeated in the House of Commons on a vote over proposed new rules for Commonwealth citizens. These rules implied that members of the EEC would have priority of entry rights over members of the old Commonwealth. In practice it has proved almost impossible to eliminate the White Commonwealth, and British law invented a new word, 'patrial', to refer to those old Commonwealth members who had preferential rights on account of their kinship to British people over members of the new Commonwealth.

However, even the old Commonwealth countries have at times found it difficult to agree on all matter. In 1956 at the time of the Suez incident, the Canadians were dismayed at the prospect of British intervention in Egypt. It was, as one of them put it, 'like finding a beloved uncle arrested for rape'. Australians too are often exasperated by British formality which they contrast with the easy social *mores* of the Australian scene. In 1973 there was clear evidence that even the easy relations were not to be taken for granted and the Australian Attorney-General made reference to the largely atrophied powers of the British Crown as 'relics of colonialism' (despite the fact that the Statute of Westminster was then over forty years old).

In large part the old Dominions were settled by British workers, adventurers, and missionaries rather than members of the nobility. In consequence the old Dominions developed into energetic communities but totally devoid of an aristocratic caste. Nevertheless, British norms have been widely admired and copied and the 'middle classes' in the Dominions have frequently been described as more British than the British. The relative lack of gentility has frequently been bemoaned; knighthood was at least as highly prized in the Dominions as in Britain. One of the remarkable features in the social life of the Dominions, however, is the prevalence of what has been called 'working-class authoritarianism'. The term refers to the social attitudes of the working class and points out that it is inclined to be intolerant, nationalistic, tough rather than tender on difficult social questions. Both the Australian and South African Labour Parties have taken tough stances on race. The 'poor whites' have always been a difficult social problem in all transplanted Anglo-Saxon countries.

Most of the independent Commonwealth countries have abandoned all Constitutional and legal links with the British crown, Parliament and judiciary, and even where some powers do exist they are few and minor. Section 4 of the Statute of Westminster states:

> No Act of Parliament of the United Kingdom passed after the commencement of this Act shall extend, or be deemed to extend, to a Dominion as part of the law of that Dominion, unless it is expressly declared in that Act that the Dominion has requested, and consented to, the enactment thereof.[11]

Several countries (as of January 1975) still use the appeals procedure to the Judicial Committee of the Privy Council from their own High Courts, and these include New Zealand, Malaysia, Singapore, certain West Indian countries as well as the remaining colonies. Australia's decision to discontinue its usage of the Judicial Committee from 1973 brought the discussion of the problem into sharper focus, because Australia's new Labour Government saw its role vis-à-vis Britain as one designed to reassert Australian independence and, in so doing, dusting off the British cobwebs.

The Judicial Committee of the Privy Council is an important residuary of Empire and it still exercises a wide jurisdiction covering some twenty Commonwealth nations and territories. It was still possible therefore as late as 1973 for the Privy Council to override the Australian High Court in a tax case and to be faced with new difficult cases such as deciding whether an unborn child can sue for damages. The six states of Australia, unlike the Canadian provinces are still sovereign bodies. They may therefore technically appeal to the Privy Council, but only on legal issues outside federal law. Yet rather than abolish totally all connection with a higher court of appeal, a number of Commonwealth countries proposed an alternative Commonwealth court which could perform similar useful functions. The major difference would be that it would not be essentially a British court.

The Commonwealth still appears to suffer from what might be

described as the residual problems of Empire. For example, the rights of Commonwealth citizens (British *subjects*) to enter Britain were quite severely limited (except, for example, in the case of Uganda Asians), but rights of entry are freely extended to 'Europeans', as members of the EEC.

Within the old Commonwealth then, the forces of nationalism operate quite as strongly as they do within the new Commonwealth. The choice facing the old Commonwealth is that of discovering whether the old transnational relationships based on kith and kinship with Great Britain constitute a more solid basis for political cohesion than do nationalist tendencies. There is also the further need to discover whether pro-British positions taken up in Canada, Australia and New Zealand are anything more than internal political manoeuvrings between groups, or whether the Dominions are still 'united by a common recognition of the Queen as the symbol of their free association and, as such, the Head of the Commonwealth'.

The Caribbean Commonwealth

We include the Commonwealth Caribbean members in this chapter because they have had several centuries of association with Great Britain, an association originally based on sugar and slaves. In the Caribbean area we speak of the Commonwealth members as the Big Four: Jamaica, Guyana, Barbados, Trinidad and Tobago; the Little Six: Antigua, Dominica, Grenada, St Kitts-Nevis-Anguilla, St Lucia, St Vincent, as well as Monserrat and British Honduras, and also the Cayman, Virgin and Turks and Caicos Islands.

Most of the larger Commonwealth Caribbean states are independent; most of the smaller states are not, and there are great variations in wealth and population. Jamaica and Trinidad possess between them three-quarters of the wealth and also about three-quarters of the population. The great problem for these states is one of identity, that of knowing where they belong – to the worldwide Commonwealth of nations or to some regional grouping. The worldwide Commonwealth appears to have less meaning for the Caribbean than for many other Commonwealth members, in particular because of the remoteness of countries like Australia and New Zealand (though not Canada) which belong to the 'white' tradition, and of African states which have tended to dominate the discussions in recent years while Caribbean questions have largely been ignored at Commonwealth meetings.

There have been a number of moves since independence to find different associations in the Caribbean area to which the Commonwealth countries might attach themselves, some of which appear to be designed to discover economic relationships, and some which appear to establish closer relations with Cuba. The Caribbean Commonwealth may atrophy because it has no obvious role to play; there appears to be no positive enthusiasm for the Commonwealth but equally there is no positive movement to abandon it.

On the other hand, attempts made at local federation have not been successful. A Caribbean Free Trade Area (CARIFTA) was set up in 1971, but attempts at closer union, including federal experiments have not been previously particularly successful. During the latter period of British rule (1958-62) an attempt was made to create a Caribbean federation which failed 'because the central government was virtually powerless and its leaders were too timid'. It was at the same time 'a salt-water federation, attempting to link together islands which were scattered in a 1,500 mile area across the Caribbean, and which had little sense of community with each other'.[12]

The West Indies states appear to have preferred local political autonomy, or even some continuance of colonial rule. Jamaica and Trinidad were large enough to opt out of the federation, but the smaller territories, Antigua, St Kitts-Nevis-Anguilla, Dominica, St Lucia, Grenada and St Vincent received a form of self-government in an association with Great Britain, which retained powers and responsibilities for external and defence matters.

4 The Commonwealth in Asia

Asia is not going to be civilised after the methods of the West. There is too much Asia and she is too old.
Rudyard Kipling[1]

The association of Asian peoples with the older Dominions, predominantly European in stock, was to be, not an episode, but a continuing factor in [the Commonwealth's] history.
Nicholas Mansergh[2]

Four-fifths of the members of the Commonwealth live in Asia, principally in India, Bangladesh (formerly East Pakistan), Sri Lanka (formerly Ceylon), Malaysia, Singapore, a number of smaller semi dependent states like Brunei and a number of dependent states, notably Hong Kong.[3] These states are of course very different in a host of ways; they are different in terms of wealth, political institutions, geographical location and liking for each other. It is in Asia that Commonwealth states have fought the most bitter wars with each other; Asia is also the continent in which the Commonwealth has its poorest members. Indeed, Asia as a whole has 20 per cent of the world's land surface and 80 per cent of its population, but only 10 per cent of the world's income.

Most of the states generally follow the British-type parliamentary model though there are numerous variations, particularly as regards the role of the opposition. British influence in Asian Commonwealth states has of course declined, and by 1970 less than 10 per cent of the total administration were British trained.[4] Each of the Commonwealth Asian states has its own particular political culture which gives it a distinctive flavour, but it is interesting to note how frequently so many former British territories still cling to a framework inherited from Britain, even where this is the Sandhurst rather than the Westminster model.

Nearly all the Asian Commonwealth states are, by Western standards, economically underdeveloped and in some cases cannot exist without foreign aid. At the same time, India's population is doubling itself every twenty-five years. In India, Bangladesh and Sri Lanka, average income per head (1972 figures) is low ($115, $75, $156 respectively). Moreover, many states are primary producers and these are likely to fall in value as prices move against them. In the case of Malaysia, for example, half of the exports of the Malay peninsula are rubber. Between 1950 and 1961 rubber exports increased by 4 per cent in volume, but the revenue fell by 35 per cent.

Commonwealth countries therefore are likely to differ in many ways. It is indeed only membership of the Commonwealth itself which may differentiate one nation from another selected at random. The significance of this membership has been described previously, but in the case of Asia the various members of the Commonwealth are at least as much in competition with each other as they are in cooperation. For example, India and Hong Kong compete with each other regarding the sale of cotton and other textiles, and there is considerable rivalry between the cities of Singapore (an independent state) and Hong Kong (technically a colony) on a vast range of financial, commercial and entrepot activities. These latter two both have remarkable records in economic growth and are far removed in life-styles from the vast slow-developing areas of Commonwealth Asia.

India

India, the 'brightest jewel in the British Crown', took three centuries to fashion. Britain did not plan in advance to conquer India, and it was not until 1813 that the British government actually gave sovereignty to the actions of its subjects operating the East India Company on the sub-continent. Of course, it had been clear that British rule was already being developed in India and legislation was approved in 1773 and 1784. The great statesmen Edmund Burke put the point well when he said that 'in fact the East India Company in India is a State in the disguise of a merchant'.

It is customary and commonplace to deride and denounce imperialism and colonialism, and without doubt there were many aspects of British rule which some Indians found oppressive, but there is also a credit side to be considered. British rule made modern India possible. Concepts such as parliamentary institutions, a government based on law and 'the greatest happiness of the greatest number' became possible, if not always realised. The British introduced modern science and built roads, harbours and railways, and connected the whole subcontinent with postal and telegraph services. Western education was provided for, though its method of implementation has its critics. Also on the 'credit' side, many traditional features of Indian life were undisturbed, though in certain instances British rule involved the termination of customs which to Western eyes were repugnant. The two most famous examples are *suttee,* the practice of the burning of widows on the funeral pyre of their dead husbands, and *thuggee,* the practice of ritual strangulation.

Western ethical standards, which both for good and for ill, penetrated India slowly in the early years of the raj, gradually became more pervasive as India felt the full impact of western ideas. Perhaps the greatest vehicle for change was the spread of the use of the English language, which while it unified India with one major tongue simultaneously opened up a world of ideas to the Indian intellectual elite.

At the same time (and somewhat paradoxically) Englishmen in India after the 1850s, grew lax in their efforts to understand Indian life, customs and languages. The Indian mutiny (1857) was in part caused because sepoys (Muslim soldiers) were required to use cartridges which had been coated with animal fat, an unclean, even sacrilegious, act. The raj was shown to be vulnerable even though it took ninety years to remove it completely.

Between 1600 and 1900, the population of India grew from about 100 million to 300 million and India enjoyed paternalistic, efficient and generally honest tutelage. Yet it was the paternalism (or rather maternalism) of the late Victorian era which irritated the Indian elite. Victoria became Empress of India in 1877 for largely theatrical reasons, inspired by Disraeli's rather flamboyant style. In 1910 King George V visited India in great pomp and splendour, but by then the Indian empire had entered a period of rapid decline.

Indian nationalism provided the most effective if not the only challenge to British rule. The Indian Congress Party met from 1885 with the support of a number of private Englishmen, but in the 1890s the nationalists drew strength from the resentment stimulated by the regime of the Viceroy, Lord Curzon, who tightened control over the Indian universities and divided up the Bengal Province for administrative convenience. The Muslims created their Muslim League in 1906. At the same time a series of natural disasters greatly increased the problems of day-to-day administration.

From the time of the Morley-Minto reforms of 1909, which involved a greater element of Indian consultation, the British could grant only further concessions. In 1929 Great Britain announced a determination to lead India to Dominion status, and in 1935 proposed a constitution to provide some greater measure of provincial reform, but this was delayed by the outbreak of war in 1939.

In 1942 the British government sent Sir Stafford Cripps to India to offer a further advance, but the mission failed largely because of mutual distrust among different religious and cultural groups; at the same time Indians could see that a greater prize could be obtained. 'Sir Stafford Cripps', said the wife of the Secretary of State, 'is like the Dove that Noah sent out from the Ark. He is constantly going out making contacts, but up till now finding no solid ground.' The prize was full national independence which was gained on 15 August, 1947. Independence involved partition into India and Pakistan whose subsequent post-independence relations will be discussed later.

At the time of independence, India's population was about 390 million; by 1971 (census figure) it was about 547 million. The population of India is growing each year by about 2.5 per cent, about 12 to 13 million persons annually. *Every day* India's population will increase by 40,000 persons and the likelihood is that India's population will equal that of China by about the year 2000 with both at 1000 million.

Caste-bound Hindus constitute about 85 per cent of the population, but they in their turn are subdivided into a complex network of smaller groups and castes. The Muslims living in India (as distinct from those living in Pakistan) constitute about 12 per cent and they too, are divided, although occasionally they unite when militant Hindus threaten. India also has important minorities of Christians, Sikhs, Buddhists and Jains, as well as areas of non-Hindu tribal peoples.

The peoples of India have considerable problems of communication, of feeding themselves and of procuring meaningful employment for their ever-growing numbers.

India is a vast country in size with seven cities of over a million inhabitants, 107 cities of more than 100,000, some 3,000 cities of fewer than 100,000 and more than half a million villages. Fifteen major languages are spoken as well as many minor languages and thousands of regional dialects; in addition, the British established English as the major vehicle of communication. In the 1961 Census there were 1,652 mother tongues to be counted as well as 826 distinct languages of which 14 were spoken as mother tongues by nearly 90 per cent of the population. About half of the population understands some variant of Hindu. The task of feeding India's huge population is immense. Agriculture already accounts for nearly 56 per cent of India's national income, but even with better farming methods and rice yields, India cannot feed all her population and needs to import 10-12 million tons of food each year. At the same time the country is confronted by a daunting problem of unemployment.

In order to grasp something of the problems of employing the millions of young Indians who are looking for work, we should contrast India's employment situation with that of another Commonwealth country, New Zealand. The contrast between employment patterns in India and New Zealand could not be more marked. We might consider the following facts.

figures in millions

	India	*New Zealand*
Population	550 (est)	2.8
Working Population	226	1.6
Persons at work	113 (50%)	1.59 (99.9%)

On the one hand India is under severe strains to find jobs for the people, of whom 110 million are in any case (under) employed in agriculture, while on the other hand, New Zealand is often unable to find suitable people for the jobs.

The mobilisation of these many groups has proved to be a difficult operation. To obtain some insight into this problem one might contrast India's approach to social change with that of China under the Cultural Revolution. If Mao Tse-tung had been born in India, it has been said, and had imposed the Cultural Revolution there, he would have shaken India from many of its complacent attitudes. He would no doubt have requested those of highborn princely caste to accept on invitation at bayonet point to spend the rest of their lives in the most menial of dirty tasks. Those refusing would have been killed. Indian vegetarians would have been compelled to eat meat as a prerequisite for any job whatsoever. All religions would have been proscribed by Mao and the worship of his own personality established. At the same time the taxation and work systems would have been radically altered and parliamentary government entirely abolished overnight.

Communism has not 'captured' India as it has overwhelmed China. There are significant areas of India in which Communist support is to be found, though overall the total Communist vote approximates to less than 10 per cent. In West Bengal, Kerala and Andhra there are some caste communities (the Ezhavas and Kammas) who support Communist Naxalbari candidates though both left and right wings are to be found. The group known as the Naxalites (from the Naxalbari district of West Bengal) were a more difficult problem for the Indian government, for they actually organised themselves for Maoist type direct action, including land occupation. However, India struggles along with partial and piecemeal systems neither quite in or outside either the capitalist or socialist camp.

In a country as vast and complex as India one would not expect to find a simple political unitary structure. In effect, India is a federal-type state because of its very size and each of the twenty-one states, except Nagaland, has a population exceeding those of many of the nations of Asia. In 1949, at the time of the enactment of the Indian Constitution, there were 562 princely states. These were merged with the other units of British India to form twenty-seven new states. Even these states had arbitrary boundaries, and in 1956 a fresh start was made to draw boundaries according to language divisions. The fourteen states then created were of equal rank. They were: Andhra Pradesh, Assam, Bihar, Bombay, Jammu and Kashmir, Kerala, Madhya Pradesh, Madras, Mysore, Orissa, Punjab, Rajasthan, Uttar Pradesh, and West Bengal. In addition, six centrally administered territories were created: Andaman and Nicobar Islands, Delhi, Himachal Pradesh, Laccadive and Amindivi Islands, Manipur, and Tripura. Technically, and according to Article 1 of the Constitution, India is a 'Union of States'.

Hindi was the dominant language in Uttar Pradesh, Bihar and Madhya Pradesh; two languages related to Hindi, Rajasthani and Punjabi, prevailed in Rajasthan and the Punjab. Kashmiri prevailed in the Vale of Kashmir. Telugu, Tamil, Bengali, Kannada, Malayalam, Oriya and Assamese predominated in the states of Andra Pradesh, Madras (Tamil Nadu), West Bengal, Mysore, Kerala, Orissa and Assam respectively.

Since 1956 new states have been created as well as a number of centrally administered territories such as the former Portuguese and French colonies of Goa and Pondicherry. Yet further divisions, additions and subtractions have taken place largely concerning language and regional sentiment, for example in Bombay, Himachal Pradesh and Assam. Separation is never far from the scene and regionalism is especially powerful in Andra Pradesh and the old Madras state. Nobody can really discover the best basic unit or size and so define India other than as (to use the cliché) a 'geographical expression'.

A particularly difficult situation is to be found in Nagaland, a small area between eastern India and Burma. In 1947 the British gave Nagaland to India, in spite of the demands of the Nagas for independence. However, India attempted to incorporate the Nagas as the smallest state in the Indian Union. Although India has attempted to compromise by granting every concession short of actual statehood (which it dare not do for fear of encouraging other states to secede), Naga nationalism has remained unsatisfied. In 1972 an attempt was made on the life of the Chief Minister of Nagaland and India unilaterally broke a ceasefire agreement made in 1964.

The Nagas have accused the Indian army of pillage, rape and torture, but India has firmly refused to allow independent observers into Nagaland to investigate these charges. The conclusion which was drawn by the investigation carried on by the Minority Rights Group, which examines the positions of groups suffering discrimination, is that India cannot expect to be exonerated from the charges unless she allows access to independent opinion.

The Constitution of India was enacted on 26 November, 1949 as a 'sovereign, democratic republic', devoted to the ideals of justice, liberty, equality, and fraternity. The body of the document consists of 395 articles and eight schedules and is possibly the most comprehensive constitutional document in the world, setting out, as well as normal constitutional bodies such as presidency and Parliament, detailed civil rights and directive principles of state policy which included amongst other things, the prohibition of intoxicating drinks, drugs and the slaughter of cows.

The first elections were held in late 1951. Most of the 174 million electors were illiterate, so the mounting of the elections was a minor miracle. The Congress Party won these elections, taking 363 of the 489 seats in the Lok Sabha or 'House of the People'. Subsequent elections were held in 1957, 1962, 1967 and 1971 and in these the Congress Party has always won an overall majority of seats, although by the late 1960s it had lost a great deal of its early appeal for a number of reasons, including the severe split in the party in 1969 which led to the expulsion of Mrs Gandhi, the Prime Minister, from her own party.[5]

In the election of 1971 Mrs Gandhi gained a landslide victory for her policies of moderate socialism. Her section of the Congress Party received 350 seats in the Lok Sabha, though the party gained only 43 per cent of the popular vote. The opposition Congress Party won sixteen seats, and the Communists twenty-four. The Jan Sangh Party, campaigned on the issue of a nationwide law to prohibit the slaughter of cattle, but attracted slight electoral support.

The Congress Party had come to power as the vehicle of independence, yet nearly thirty years after independence no issue as large and compellingly cohesive as independence from Great Britain had emerged in Indian politics. Perhaps India's problems are too immense to permit of their solution by the mechanics of party politics.

One useful approach to the understanding of the complexities of Indian politics is to speak of the various styles or idioms which are commonly found in Indian political life. We may perhaps enumerate them as follows:

1 The 'saintly' idiom. India owes her eventual independence from Britain to the efforts of millions of Indians, but above all to the character and personality of Mohandas Karamchand Gandhi.[6] He may be said to represent the 'saintly' strand in Indian politics, still an important tendency, though becoming less so. Gandhi made his reputation in South Africa, where he became the champion of the rights of the Indian community. His political ideas formed during this period, they were a mixture of Gujarati and Tolstoyan philosophies, and rested on the belief that non-violence was the highest morality. Coupled with this was a fierce antipathy to Western society as being materialistic. He elaborated these ideas, adding to them his own notion of *satya* (truth). Gandhi's power lay in the fact that his own saintly life together with his understanding of Hindu aspirations gave him unique political power. By preaching simplicity and independence from the West he appealed to millions of his countrymen. The fundamentalist idealist is always a powerful opponent; when he is also a dedicated tactician he is frequently unbeatable. Gandhi made the national independence struggle into a mass movement, or as one writer put it, 'he nationalised nationalism'.

If Gandhi was India's *prophet* (until his death in 1947) Nehru was *leader* until his death in 1965. Nehru's first hope in the 1920s was of course for independence, but in the longer run he wanted to create a self-sufficient and dignified India not 'a cheap and inefficient replica of the countries of the West'. Imperialism and capitalism were for him grown from the same plant. He therefore opposed both the British Empire and its offspring, industrialism. He mistrusted international trade and placed his faith in economic planning. The results of this policy are evident today. There is in India an ambivalent attitude to economic change; there is hostility towards private enterprise yet not enough realism regarding the proven limitations of economic planning.

2 The 'modern' idiom. Great men are frequently unable or unwilling to cope with the humdrum problems of organising a party or movement. The great goals which they set for themselves are often not easily attainable, particularly in the hands of lesser men. The second element in Indian politics may be described as the *modern* organisational politics of the Congress Party with its splits, schisms, bargains and compromises. Modern politics is of course the politics of New Delhi and the big towns and this does not basically touch the lives of countless millions of Indians who live in villages.

3 The 'village' idiom. The third aspect of Indian politics therefore is the life of village politics. The idiom of village politics is that of small peasant producers who eke out a precarious living. This political idiom is not that of the big towns with its sophisticated style of living, rather it is the micropolitics of a million small decisions and of the decision-makers. For these people the habit of voting is perhaps insufficiently understood, or where it is understood it is structured on the family or extended family.[7] We might further describe this situation as face-to-face politics, in which people deal with each other as people and not through bureaucracies or representatives. The dominant characteristics of the village idiom are status, custom and a relatively undeveloped amount of specialisation. Traditionally, Indian political life has been a village life because India is a nation of 550,000 villages in which live more than 80 per cent of the population. Village life is of course narrowly circumscribed and even today the world of the average villager extends only a few miles beyond the place of his birth. Modern communications, including radio, mobile film units and increasing contact with state officials have broken down a few of the old barriers. However, village life is largely a static life in which the traditional caste system is tenaciously maintained. Castes rarely intermarry, dress differently, and will not normally eat together.

Writing in the London *Times* in 1973, an Indian journalist Sarwar Lateef argued that from 1945 to 1972.

> Indo-British relations at the political level were rather unhealthy, and quite often unhappy. The attitudes of the two countries to each other were influenced by what may be described as colonial hangups; a kind of love-hate relationship based upon feelings of guilt and sentimentality rather than a cool assessment of mutual interests.[8]

Between India and Britain, the one-time imperial power, not much more than historical memories remain. For example, trading relations show a steady and persistently sharp decline. In 1960-61, India imported from Britain goods to the value of £163 million. By 1971 this figure had dropped to £70 million. As for India's exports the decline over the same ten-year period was from £129 million to £94 million. The proportion of imports into India from Britain fell from 20 per cent to 7.7 per cent, while the proportion of India's exports sent to Britain fell from 27 per cent to 11 per cent. India's exports constitute only 1 per cent of the British market. Who has taken Britain's place? The answer is, in short, the Soviet Union, which apart from having negotiated a treaty of friendship with India has also become a most important source of imports and exports–over one-fifth in all

At the same time, Britain's *political* influence in India steadily declined after 1947, so much so that India could fight one war with China and four with Pakistan and enter into a close military relationship with the Soviet Union without any British involvement. Britain could even witness the dismembership of her creation, Pakistan, without much comment – in fact British attitudes were those of sympathy for India. In an article written by Mrs Indira Gandhi, the Indian Prime Minister, in late 1972, 'India and the World' hardly any mention was made of Britain at all, though much was said about the role of the USA, the Soviet Union and China.

Britain's relative decline as a world power, and her adherence to the EEC took her further and further away from India so that little except memories of British rule remained. By the 1970s Britain was much more concerned about Indians who had been established in Africa. Nevertheless British aid to India continues at a sum of about £40 million per annum, and British investment in India is still considerable. Indo-British relations in short may be described as orderly, beneficial, businesslike and generally conducted without bitterness.

India has been at war with her neighbour Pakistan on four occasions since independence. The origins of these bitter relations are to be perceived deep into Indian history, and were only temporarily 'settled' with the creation of Pakistan, in 1947. Little was finally settled and the dispute over certain areas like Kashmir continued for many years.

Nehru, the first Indian Prime Minister once remarked: 'There are only two forces in India today, British imperialism and Indian nationalism as represented by the Congress.' To this remark, the Muslim leader

Mahammed Ali Jinnah replied: 'No, there is a third party, the Muslims.' In 1940 Jinnah stated that Hindus and Muslims formed two separate nations. Muslim nationalism eventually achieved its goal with the creation in 1947 of a separate and independent Islamic state, Pakistan, simultaneously with India's achievement of independence.

India's hostility to Pakistan derives from a number of factors. The first of course is cultural and religious. The Muslims and Hindu religions are at variance with each other on a number of matters loosely termed 'cultural'. To the Muslim the sword has always been a necessary element in the defence of his religion, and the concept of the holy war (*Jehad*) has implied a refusal to compromise on fundamental beliefs. To the Hindu tolerance simply means accommodation to the 'facts'.

The second may be loosely called 'political' in the sense that Indians have often reacted scornfully to Pakistan's military politics. Since 1956, most of the time Pakistan has been a military state, though it has had three shortlived constitutions. Pakistan, as befits a Muslim state, believes that power flows from God. As a theocratic state it accepts certain goals as right, such as the simple quasi-authoritarian goals implicit in the Muslim faith. India, on the other hand, argues that political power flows in principle from the people (as outlined in her Constitution) and claims to be a democratic state. India also claims to be a secular state: it has no official state religion.

Both India and Pakistan, however, have great difficulties with centrifugal or secessionist tendencies. One writer said that 'Pakistanis are a people united by a common will to be a nation, but they do not yet know what kind of nation they wish to be'.[9] India has to cope with a vast variety of cultural, religious and linguistic pressures. Both states present political paradoxes. Pakistan upholds a conception of revolution and utopianism but all within a strictly conservative framework. India's official state policy is to promote and protect social equality, but the continued operation of the caste-lobby system inhibits the process.

Speaking in March 1940, M. A. Jinnah, the founder of independent Pakistan put the Pakistani viewpoint as follows.

> They may be said indeed to represent two distinct and separate civilisations. Hinduism is distinguished by the phenomenon of caste, which is the basis of its religions and social system, and, save in a very restricted field, remains unaffected by contact with the philo-

sophies of the West, the religion of Islam, on the other hand, is based upon the conception of the equality of man.

He went on to say that these differences 'govern not only his law and culture but every aspect of his social life, and such religions, essentially exclusive, completely preclude that merging of identity and unity of thought on which Western democracy is based'.

In 1971 East Pakistan broke away from Pakistan and created the new state of Bangladesh (Bengal land). Bangladesh was admitted to the Commonwealth and West Pakistan left it. India supported Bangladesh and sent in her army to help the East Bengalis to drive out the West Pakistan army which had invaded the East and put down the 'rebellion' there with great cruelty.

Pakistan was originally created with two wings, West and East, but they were separated by 1,000 miles of territory and represented in fact two distinct cultures. East Bengal (East Pakistan) was a South-east Asian country of monsoon rains and rice, whose people are short and dark with a strong cultural affinity with other Bengalis living in India itself. West Pakistan is essentially a middle-eastern country, partly desert, partly wheat-growing, whose people appear to have military inclinations and a desire to dominate their eastern neighbours. Indeed as the former President Ayub Khan put it, 'an average East Pakistani in Dacca thought that the West Pakistani officials were a manifestation of colonialism'.

In December 1970 the Awami League of East Pakistan decisively won the second election in Pakistan's history. The leader of the Awami League, Sheik Mujib Rahman, obtained 72 per cent of the East Pakistan vote and all but two of the seats in the legislature. What was started as an internal party discussion, resulted in full-scale war involving three parties, the West Pakistan army (at that time the Pakistan army), the seceding state of East Bengal and the forces of India (which received ten million destitute refugees).

India's position was simple. Pakistan denied 'basic human values' and was 'a ruthless military dictatorship', to use the words of Mrs Gandhi, which was 'totally alienated from its own people'. The attitude of President Bhutto, appointed after the event, did not suggest that he disagreed fundamentally with this viewpoint. On 27 June, 1972 he said:

> The war we have lost was not of our making. I had warned against it but my warning fell on deaf ears of a power-drunk junta. They

recklessly plunged our people into the war and involved us in an intolerable surrender and lost us half our country. The junta did not know how to make peace nor did it know how to make war.

Eventually India and Pakistan concluded the Simla Agreement of 2 July, 1972, by which it was resolved that disputes between the two should not be settled by force. Pakistan became a smaller state still subjected to secessionist pressures on its western flank, as in Baluchistan, but it left the Commonwealth.

The strange interplay of the great powers in India and Pakistan should be noted. The Soviet Union and the United Kingdom supported India, while China and the United States supported Pakistan. The posture adopted by China was of great significance. Any Asian problem which appears to have India on one side, has China and Pakistan on the other, and President Bhutto clearly stipulated that 'Pakistan will always need a plus-factor for coping with India. . . . it so happens that the plus-factor is the People's Republic of China. If that factor is removed, Pakistan will always be at the mercy of all the three great powers and India.'

What are the main lessons for the Commonwealth? In the first place, the relative unimportance of the power which once controlled the large destinies of India testifies to the total disappearance of the British raj, or indeed of any meaningful influence. In the second place, the Commonwealth itself appears to have been powerless to prevent two of its members from fighting a bitter war in the Indian subcontinent (as it has been equally powerless in the conflicts in Nigeria, Cyprus and Ceylon). The powers involved called upon other non-Commonwealth powers to support their particular causes in wars which became rapidly international rather than Commonwealth. India was immersed in Asian affairs. Indeed apart from Pakistan, her major problem has been to come to terms with the new China with whom she fought an expensive war over tracts of desolate, difficult and useless territory'.[10]

Sri Lanka

In February 1948 the new Dominion of Ceylon was born, not as in the case of India and Pakistan as a Republic, but as a state owing allegiance to the British Crown. Ceylon was conquered by Britain in 1796 and the central kingdom of Kandy, which had succeeded in maintaining its independence of the Portuguese, Dutch and British, finally accepted British suzerainty in 1815. The link with the British crown lasted 157 years.

The Republic of Sri Lanka was inaugurated on 22 May, 1972 when a new constitution was introduced to replace that of Ceylon. In accordance with the terms of the constitution, the Prime Minister, Mrs Sirinavo Bandaranaike, continued in office, while the Governor-General became the first President. This constitution clearly spelt out the official status of the Sinhala language. Tamil, spoken by about 20 per cent of the population, was catered for by special provisions. Special status was granted to Buddhism as the religion of the majority of people, but this was not meant to preclude freedom of religious observance.

The creation of a Republic of Sri Lanka was envisaged in 1970 when the United Front Coalition came into office. This coalition comprised Mrs Bandaranaike's Sri Lanka's Freedom Party in alliance with the Communist Party and the Trotskyist Lanka Sama Samaja Party. Arguments developed about the 1972 Constitution which, the members of the opposition argued, placed too much power in the hands of the political party in office and downgraded the judiciary. The Tamil (Federal) party complained that the Tamil language and the Tamil-speaking community was given insufficient recognition in the new republic. Sri Lanka's difficulties form part of a common Asian problem of communalism. All Asian communities face 'dilemmas of statehood' of this sort, but Sri Lanka faced a particularly formidable combination of problems, communal, religious, racial and economic.

Sri Lanka's political issues are immediately perceptible in the areas of race and language. These are most in evidence in the north and east of the country. The north is almost exclusively a Tamil area, the east very largely so, and in these parts of the country the situation has been almost continuously explosive. Potential 'plots' are frequently discovered.

Since 1956, when Mrs Bandaranaike's husband, S. W. R. D. Bandaranaike came to power on a platform of 'Sinhalese language, religion and race in danger', the north and east have been in perpetual turmoil. For most of her first period in office (1960-65) Mrs Bandaranaike ruled these turbulent regions 'out of the barrel of a gun'.

Although Tamils are permitted to communicate with the government and may educate their children in Tamil, many young Tamils feel that they are of importance to the government only at election time. They have become increasingly frustrated and have advocated the creation of a separate Tamil state, by force if necessary. Their minimum demand is for the setting up of an autonomous Tamil province within a federation.

The Sri Lanka government is unlikely to agree either to political or more purely linguistic demands. To accept the Tamil demand for linguistic equality is probably tantamount to committing political suicide. The Sinhalese government draws its strength from the Sinhalese electorate of 10 million and could never accept the Tamil claims. Language is the burning issue because it is the key to jobs, and in an economy of high unemployment, jobs are difficult to obtain. At the same time the economy is bedevilled by acute inflation, increasing demands on its meagre output, and depleted reserves of foreign exchange.

Deep and ideological internecine conflicts developed in Ceylon in the wake of Mrs Bandaranaike's victories. Once in office, there emerged a Maoist group known as the JVP (Janata Vinukti Peramuna, People's United Front), which challenged the political credibility of Mrs Bandaranaike as a leader of the Left and of Buddhist nationalism. So complicated did the left-wing political spectrum become that both the Ceylon Communist Party and the Trotskyite groups came to be regarded as part of the Establishment. The JVP entirely rejected the parliamentary process and sought to bring down the government by violent means.

The future fortunes of the young state may depend on its taking more moderate and less revolutionary courses of action. These were already suggested in 1971. Thus although one of the government's first acts was to grant recognition to North Korea, the North Koreans were deported; at the same time, while Sri Lanka attacked Singapore's continued use of the British base in Singapore, the Government was compelled to accept arms to suppress the JVP uprising. Insurgency was an intractable problem but could hardly be fought unless more was spent on defence, with a consequent depletion of economic resources devoted to other areas. The political crises of Sri Lanka could be solved only with very careful management, judiciously made concessions and a great deal of good luck.

Malaysia and Singapore

As early as the thirteenth century, Malays inhabiting the coasts of what are now Malaya, Sarawak and Sabah established small trading ports and traded with early European traders and adventurers. It was the lure of spices and the fortune which they brought in their wake which attracted these early traders to the East Indies. The Portuguese were followed by the Dutch and the British, who found it expedient to take control of the various territories so that they could protect their enterprises from each other. In 1511 the Portuguese occupied Malacca, with its strategic position on the west coast of Malaya, and in 1592 the British East India Company established itself at Penang.

Singapore, which is today an island to the south of the Malay peninsula, was originally a mangrove swamp. Through the efforts of Sir Stamford Raffles, the farseeing pioneering agent of the British East India Company, a thriving city was created; this became the world's fifth port and a highly prized part of the British Empire. The three territories of Penang, Malacca and Singapore were established as the Straits Settlement in 1867.

North Borneo (Sabah), Sarawak and Brunei were declared British protectorates in 1888. Between 1909 and 1914, British Malaya was further extended to take in the four states to the north and Johore in the extreme south. The whole area was reconstructed in 1945 in order to create the union of Malaya by uniting Penang and Malacca with the nine Malay states; Singapore, Sabah and Sarawak become crown colonies. In 1948 the Union of Malaya was succeeded by the Federation of Malaya. At the same time, however, Malaya entered a twelve-year period of insurrection and insurgency as the ethnic Chinese groups, inspired by Communist successes elsewhere in Asia, attempted to overthrow the regime.

The federation of Malaysia was formed in September 1963, but one of its constituent units, Singapore, left the Federation in August 1965. Since 1965, Malaysia has come to consist of Malaya (which is a modernising state) and the two Borneo territories of Sarawak and Sabah. In economic terms, Malaysia enjoys an average income per head of about US$428 (1972), which is high for the South-east Asian region. In spite of Japanese occupation (1942-45), and a disruptive Communist revolt (1948-60), followed by a bitter 'confrontation' with a prickly Indonesia under the erratic President Sukarno, Malaysia has prospered.

The major problems of Malaysia are economic and racial, both of which colour local politics. The economy rests on a very narrow base. The federation is a major producer of rubber, which has a fluctuating world price, and of tin, which is likely to become increasingly expensive to mine. About one-third of the gross national product is derived from agriculture, and about 12 per cent from manufacturing. Economic progress has been made, by the use of five-year plans, but this can only be sustained by the diversification of crops and by industrialisation. Malaya itself is commercially progressive, but Sarawak and Sabah have made slow progress since independence. Yet as we have already seen in the case of Sri Lanka, economic, political, communal and linguistic problems are very closely interrelated.

The fundamental racial issue in Malaysia can be simply stated; there exist two contrasting groups, the Muslim Malays and the ethnic Chinese, whose life styles involve a clash of temperament and of policy. The Malays form a numerical majority but the Chinese constitute the driving force in commerce, engineering and medicine.

The word 'Malay', refers to a person of the Malay race, but the word 'Malayan' refers to a person of any race, including those Chinese who reside in Malaysia. The Malays regard themselves as villagers (and even those who live in towns may return there in due course). The Malays regard themselves moreover as the indigenous owners of the land and draw their cultural strength from that fact as well as from their distinctive muslim faith. During the past century there have been many changes in Malay society with the spread of education and modernisation.[11]

About 44 per cent of the population of 10 million are Malays; as many as 36 per cent are Chinese. The rest are Indians (10 per cent) and non-Malays (10 per cent). Chinese businessmen effectively control 90 per cent of the Federation's commercial outlets. While the Malays have an aptitude and inclination for administrative and governmental work, they are at a great disadvantage in trade and commerce. Over more than a century, therefore, great resentments have built up. Chinese immigrants into Malaysia have worked hard, for example, at dangerous and dirty work in the tin mines, they have tended to organise self-help associations, and have drawn further apart from the Malays because of apparent clannishness. Malaysia rapidly developed the problems of a multiracial community.

Unlike the Malays the Chinese were not unduly interested in the operations of government because they largely approved of a laissez-faire government which does not interfere in business activities. A rough division of labour therefore emerged in which the Chinese controlled the economy and the Malays, through their slight overall numerical majority, controlled political life. Further, Malaysia became a federation in which the components showed a marked variation in Chinese ethnic strength.[12] Consequently Malays came to use their political power to ensure Malay predominance on the bare majoritarian principle. The situation is highly reminiscent of that found in Northern Ireland.

Politics in Malaysia stems from largely communal differences; though economics has also added the complications of wealth and class.[13] The British desired Malayan unity for strategic, economic and administrative reasons, The desire of Malays to protect their communal position, however, consolidated Malay nationalism. The same reasons – strategy, economics and administration – impelled Singapore into the Malay political association.

These are the forces which impelled unity, but those which have created discord are more insistent. There are significant economic and racial contrasts between the Malay states and Singapore, deriving from the fact that the latter's overwhelming Chinese population would tilt the balance in such a way that a Malaysia *including* Singapore would have a numerical majority of Chinese, but a Malaysia *excluding* Singapore has a numerical minority of Chinese. The two Borneo states were also significantly different and apprehensive.

Malay nationalism expressed itself in the UMNO (the United Malay National Organisation). The Chinese responded in two ways; firstly, they formed the MCP (Malayan Communist Party) which provided the political fuel for the Emergency of 1948-60; secondly, they formed the MCA (Malayan Chinese Association). A multiracial coalition was created which was an alliance of UMNO plus the MCA and the MIC (Malayan Indian Congress), but underneath communal loyalties were still strong. For example, the PMIP (Pan-Malayan Islamic Party) on the right of UMNO demanded that Chinese should be excluded from political rights, while the Socialist Front denounced the 'special rights' of Malays. The Alliance, as it was called, successfully controlled Malaysian politics until 1969, after which it became clear that its support among Malays was diminishing.

In May 1969 Malaysia's third post-independence general election was held. This resulted in the loss of seats for the more moderate Malay and Chinese parties (UMNO and MCA) in favour of the more nationalist group, including the PMIP and radical Chinese party, the DAP (Democratic Action Party). The alliance between the UMNO and MCA which had governed Malaysia for many years did not survive the election and the new government had no Chinese ministers. Severe rioting developed, resulting in 150 deaths and the injury of about 4,000 people.

Malaysia's multiracial coalition in effect came to an end in May 1969 with the riots and the Prime Minister, Tunku Abdul Rahman declared that 'democracy was dead' in Malaysia. A political scientist might make two comments about this remark. First, he might say that what Malaysia lacked was not 'democracy' but 'legitimacy', and that Malaysia was not a state which all races could accept as stable and acceptable. Instead, the violence of 1969 demonstrated that in Asia, elections are frequently unedifying, corrupt and even violently disruptive occasions. Secondly, Malaysia has not evolved a pattern of transcommunal interests which can transcend the more obvious racial cleavages. A 'bargain' between Chinese and Malays was struck in the form of the Alliance but the 'bargain' admitted of cleavages which linked up economic function on the one hand and political roles with race. The one possible answer appeared to some to be in the adoption of a conscious programme of modernisation in which these differences would 'wither away'.[14] These hopes have not been realised, though the next election of 1974 was carried out in a far more tranquil atmosphere than had been previously thought possible. The National Front (which consisted of 12 parties in coalition) won a decisive victory, capturing 120 out of 130 seats in the federal House of Representatives. Malaysia now saw political stability as its first essential.

Malaysian elections (for 104 seats)

	Seats (House of Representatives)		*Percentage of poll*	
	1969	*1964*	*1969*	*1964*
Alliance	66	89	48.4	58.5
of which:				
UMNO	51	59	34.2	38.4
MCA	13	27	13.0	18.6
MIC	2	3	1.2	1.5
PMIP	12	9	23.8	14.6
DAP	13	1(PAP)	13.7	2.0 (PAP)
Gerakan	8	1(UDP)	8.6	4.3(UDP)
PPP	4	2	3.9	3.4
Partai Rakyat	-	Part of SF	1.2	Part of SF
Others	-	2(SF)	0.4	17.2(SF=16.1)

Source: figures in *The Straits Times,* 12-13 May 1969.

In Malaysia the political problem has been that of balancing an 'appeal to the indigenous masses with the requirements of the economically dominant, under native elite leadership'.[15] In fact, the 'politically dominant elite of Malays, with its leaderships drawn to some extent from the families of the Malay sultans, united in the Alliance with the economically dominant Chinese'. Some form of Alliance is still a prerequisite, but the political algebra of Malaysia remains complex because 'it would seem that noncommunal parties might have some difficulty in winning a majority'.[16]

Singapore

The relationship between Singapore and Malaysia has sometimes been described as a symbiosis, which suggests that Malaysians and Singaporeans live in close proximity with each other 'neither despising the other nor acting aggressively'.

Britain developed its economic activities in nineteenth-century Malaya form Singapore, but before 1819 the marshy wastes of the latter belonged to the Johore-Lingga Kingdom. Yet Singapore does not today form a political part of the Malaysian hinterland. Economic and geographic logic suggest a merger and Singapore did form a part of Malaysia for nearly two years (August 1963 to August 1965), but since then it has become an island republic. Singapore is a tiny island of 224 square miles with no natural resources except the energy of its trading community, and an inherited network of docks, communications, facilities and port infrastructure second to none in South-east Asia.

The merger between the two states failed because the addition of a million and a half Chinese from Singapore would upset the fragile racial balance in Malaysia. At the same time, Singapore was reputedly too 'leftist' for the tastes of the Malaysian leaders. As an opposition leader, Lee Kuan Yew (now Singapore's Prime Minister) once stated that 'an island nation is a political joke', but given Singapore's continued prosperity, albeit alone and separated from its hinterland, the joke has not been unpleasant. However, the implications of the failure of the merger have been considerable.[17]

For Singapore the break involved a threat to its economic position because it could no longer be certain of free access to the markets of Malaysia and the question of unemployment was always to be considered (at times this was as high as 9 per cent). Indonesia was then hostile to Malaysia and Singapore depended on Britain for its defence.

At least one-fifth of Singapore's gross national product was derived from Britain's expenditure on troops and facilities, and these were largely withdrawn by 1972.

In the short run, Singapore's departure from Malaysia probably assisted greater political stability in both states. Neither side could be seen to be affecting the other's internal politics (as was possible for example when Singapore Chinese were accused of infiltrating Malaysian Chinese political organisations such as the Malayan Communist Party). It was in any case difficult to see how Singapore's overwhelming Chinese population could fit into the Malaysian multi-racial political pattern.

Singapore's People's Action Party (PAP) was formed in 1954 with the object of mobilising opinion against British rule. It was immediately apparent that it had two wings – the moderates and the Communists. Lee Kuan Yew emerged as the leader of the moderates and as full independence came, he used the same colonial penal laws, which he had once fought, to imprison the Communist membership. Today the PAP is firmly anti-communist and has been described as 'a calculating democratic socialist party with a non-communal structure based on a fairly homogeneous island'.[18] Singapore is 98 per cent urban, and nearly 40 per cent of the gross national product is derived from domestic and international trade. Moreover, 30 per cent of the population is engaged in finance, communications and transport enterprises. The basic problem facing Singapore is the 'close connection between the proscribed but still influential Malayan Communist Party and the main springs of Chinese national feeling'.[19] The 1955 elections produced a Labour Front which soon became the People's Action Party led by Lee Kuan Yew who has been Singapore's prime minister since the party came to power in 1959.

Singapore's politics is less 'racial' in inspiration than that of Malaysia in the sense that the members of its parties are ethnically Chinese, and more 'class'. All were originally left-wing but some more left-wing than others, so that the PAP came to power in 1959 to a large extent with the assistance of the Malayan Communist Party. Lee Kuan Yew asserted his dominance and shook off the Communist grip to establish an authoritarian regime supported by many middle-class voters. Somewhat like Kenya and the case of Kenyatta, those who feared Lee's strength subsequently sought refuge in it, as the election of 1963 showed. In the general election of 1968 the PAP won all fifty-eight seats in the Assembly; and again in 1972 an exclusively PAP Assembly (now of sixty-five seats) was returned with 70 per cent of the votes cast.

The PAP has taken its monopoly of power very seriously. It permits other parties to exist, and though only the Barisan Sosialis pose any threat there are twelve other parties operating in the territory. Lee Kuan Yew bestrides Singaporean politics like a colossus largely because he is an astute and ruthless political tactician. He has made a number of political *volte-faces:* in his time he has both tolerated and proscribed communists, western life-styles and Malaysian politicians. He has been remarkably successful by any political test, though his major successes have been largely municipal reforms, and if Singapore has 'mute conformist citizens', then this is what they want to be. There is, however, no such thing as Leekuanyewism as there has been Nkrumahism, nor any of the postcolonial ideologies associated with leaders in some young Commonwealth countries.

Hong Kong

Hong Kong has been technically a British colony since 1842 but its end may be in sight, because in 1997 the lease on the largest portion of the colony (the so-called New Territories) will expire and five-sixths of Hong Kong is then due to revert to China.[20] To explain this position we must sketch a few details about Hong Kong's political development to date.

Hong Kong island was ceded in perpetuity to the British Crown in 1842 by the Treaty of Nanking. The peninsula of Kowloon was ceded by the Convention of Peking in 1860. Kowloon is actually part of the mainland and it too was ceded as a British dependency. The case of the New Territories is quite different, because when these territories were surrendered to Britain in 1898 they were merely leased for a period of ninety-nine years. The agreement then set out was as between Queen Victoria and the Emperor of China, neither of whom could have foreseen either the dynamic growth or the turbulent history of Hong Kong in the twentieth century.

The reasons which led to the acquisition of Hong Kong in 1842 are simple. Hong Kong has a magnificent port and served as an inlet to China. In 1800 Britain supplied 4,000 chests of opium to China; by 1839 (just before the occupation of Hong Kong) this figure had risen to 39,000. Hong Kong's importance has therefore progressed in that it was first designed to careen ships, later became an entrepot port and subsequently added manufacturing, banking, financial expertise and tourism to its manifold business activities. Above all, Hong Kong has prospered because no particular political pattern has been forced on it. The Chinese believe that human conduct must not be regulated by an impersonal government but rather by the family. Hence, provided the colonial government has kept out of customary life, no fundamental objection to British rule has been raised.

Population grew from 30,000 in 1849 (28,000 of whom were Chinese) to 87,000 in 1859 to 1,500,000 in 1939, but fell during the Japanese occupation so that by 1945 the population was less than 500,000. Once British rule was restored in 1945 the rate of return was 100,000 every month and by 1950 had increased to 2,360,000 as refugees poured in after the victory of the Communist armies in China in 1949. In 1971 the population was just under 4 million, of whom all but 50,000 persons were Chinese, the vast majority of whom speak Cantonese.

There have been several grave international crises during this century. The first dates back to 1911 when the Chinese Revolution took place and the Chinese Empire crumbled before the predatory activities of the Western powers which had arbitrarily partitioned China into spheres of influence in the second half of the nineteenth century. In the 1920s there were boycotts against British goods and Hong Kong experienced severe disturbances. After the Japanese occupation from 1941 to 1945 (and largely through American pressure) it appeared likely for a while that Britain might not resume occupation. In 1949 the Chinese People's Republic was established and thus naturally involved Hong Kong and its status, particularly as 776,000 refugees crossed the border from China into Hong Kong. Finally in 1967 Hong Kong experienced severe riots which coincided with the upheaval of the Cultural Revolution inside China. On all of these occasions Hong Kong has appeared to be threatened, but has nevertheless managed to survive.

China tolerates the existence of the colony of Hong Kong, a fact even the more remarkable because China has been such an aggressive world power. The extraordinary conditions whereby China coexists with Hong Kong may be described as a situation in which '200 per cent capitalism faces 200 per cent communism'. China's basic economic gain from the existence of Hong Kong is the large amount of valuable foreign exchange.

The question which is at the heart of the problem as to whether the Chinese government (whatever that may be in 1997) will be prepared to renegotiate the lease of the New Territories on the expiration of the lease, and so presumably permit Hong Kong to remain a colony into the twenty-first century. Before attempting specifically to answer this point, it must be stated that China does not regard British occupancy of Hong Kong as indicating British sovereignty in respect of the territory. In short Hong Kong is a 'part of China' and not a 'part of Britain'. Hence China refers to the 'British authorities' in Hong Kong and not to a properly legally constituted state.

Given these somewhat contrasting attitudes it is difficult to see what is the common ground on which the problem of 1997 can be discussed. If China sees Hong Kong as under its own sovereign jurisdiction, how could she be prepared to negotiate regarding the future of her own territory? 'Sooner or later', 'when the time is ripe', Hong Kong will be reabsorbed into China. In the meantime, it is extremely profitable to China as a means of earning valuable much needed foreign exchange at the rate of £1 million per day.

Technically, Hong Kong is a colony but it would be wrong to see it as a Gold Coast struggling to become a Ghana. Hong Kong possesses one of the most sophisticated financial business and manufacturing infrastructures in the whole Commonwealth. Yet technically it is no more than a part of Britain's sovereign dominions. In fact it is misleading to use the term 'colony' with regard to Hong Kong. The Chinese authorities do not regard it as such and the British authorities know that Hong Kong is ultimately militarily indefensible as a colony. It makes much more sense to regard Hong Kong as an administrative superstructure over a thriving economic base. The year 1997 is some way off and in the meantime no one in the 1970s is unduly concerned about events in the late 1990s.

While Hong Kong is a 'colony', Singapore is an independent island republic. However, the two territories have often been compared because both began life as island trading posts and are largely peopled by ethnic Chinese from southern Asia. Both populations are largely refugee and have become experts at manufacturing and business practices. Both were occupied by the Japanese during the Second World War and both have since enjoyed very high rates of growth. Hong Kong, the colony, has grown even faster than Singapore, the independent state. Whereas in 1963 the per capita income in Hong Kong was barely half that of Singapore, by 1969 Hong Kong's per capita income had outstripped that of Singapore.

The following table of comparison may help to show the comparisons of three Asian Commonwealth states.

State	*1966* (in US$)	*1968* (in US$)
Hong Kong		
Gross national product	996 million	2,630 million
Per Capita income	324	680
Singapore		
Gross national product	717 million	1,492 million
Per capita income	438	751
Malaysia		
Gross national product	2,173 million	3,362 million
Per capita income	268	326

Both Singapore and Hong Kong have accomplished a metamorphosis from trade to industry since the end of the Second World War, and both economies have advanced rapidly. In the case of Hong Kong, about half of its gross domestic product is obtained from manufacturing, while in the case of Singapore the figure for manufacturing is 25 per cent of its gross domestic product. Singapore's growth rate is the highest in the whole Asia-Pacific region, not excluding Japan or Australia, Hong Kong's gross national product is double that of Singapore. Both are great financial centres and Hong Kong's stock exchanges in particular were involved in a greater volume of business in the first part of 1973 than London. The energy of the Commonwealth's Chinese citizens is unquestioned.

Conclusion

The Commonwealth in Asia is drawing away from the British connection. For hundreds of years Britain maintained decisive control over the destinies of millions of people in the Asian continent. Indians, Ceylonese, Chinese, Burmese, Malays, and a variety of other Asian ethnic groups. In 1947 the independence of India produced a fundamental change in the imperial politics of Asia. India became a Republic within the Commonwealth, accepting the Queen as its Head. Such a constitutional solution looked to be a piece of political chicanery at the time, but has proved to be a valuable answer to some of the problems of constitutional independence. The Asian members of the Commonwealth, however, still face a large number of difficult issues. The

Commonwealth indicates at times how much men are attached to national symbols (such as flags, anthems, badges and rank) rather than to political realities. The disputes between India and Pakistan over territorial possessions (especially over Bangladesh and Kashmir) have been severe, but both India and Pakistan face such desperate problems of feeding their populations that any prospect of war between them is cruel folly. One has the feeling that a little less concentration on status questions and rather more on agriculture and irrigation would greatly assist development. What is required is to raise 'less hell and more corn' – to invert the famous comment of the US President Harry Truman.

Many of the residual problems of Empire which particularly tax presentday Commonwealth leaders are related to the earlier migration of Asian labour. The British sent Indians as indentured labourers to places as far apart as Trinidad, Fiji, Mauritius, Natal and British Guiana.[21] Once established, Indian labourers turned themselves into Indian businessmen, particularly as commercial middlemen. In Africa, in particular, they had some of the skills which the indigenous Africans lacked, while at the same time they were not reluctant to accept small profits for their efforts, sometimes well below those for which Europeans would work. The presence of many Asians in Britain itself bears witness to the fact that displaced Indians are amongst the 'casualties of empire'.

In Malaysia and Singapore ethnic problems too have remained difficult. The industrious Chinese – 'the Jews of Asia' as they are sometimes called – have established commercial dominion in much of South-east Asia, both within and without the Commonwealth. Singapore, in particular, bears eloquent testimony to this fact, though Lee Kwan Yew's notions of morality are regarded as illiberal and old-fashioned by some progressive opinion. Hong Kong still remains a problem for the future; indeed of approximately five million persons *still* living in British dependencies and colonies, approximately 4 million are the Chinese residents of Hong Kong.

It would be wrong to imagine that Britain and the Asian Commonwealth have sundered all ties merely because the obvious imperial links have been removed. In its aid programmes in the operation of specialised agencies, and in its export of goods and services, Britain is still a very considerable influence in Asia.

5 The Commonwealth in Africa

The New African States were created by European Powers who brought together under one administration heterogeneous ethnic groups, speaking different languages, sometimes possessing distinct cultures and religions.
K. A. Busia[1]

Ex Africa semper aliquid novi (There is always something new from Africa).
Pliny, AD 23-79

A large part of geographical Africa has been under British rule at some stage. Egypt came under British control in the period 1883-1907, and in the First World War became a British protectorate. The occupation was supposed to be jointly administered by Britain and France, but French internal political difficulties left Britain as sole effective ruler. The Sudan was governed from 1899 to 1955 by a condominium of Britain and Egypt. Black Africa came into the British Empire in three stages. In the first place, British traders and merchants directed their efforts towards West Africa, in particular on account of the trade in African slaves, which during the eighteenth century made enormous profits for slave traders who transported many millions across the Atlantic to the sugar plantations of the West Indies. West Africa has therefore a long record of European commercial penetration, but not of European settlement, though of course traders and government officials lived for many years in the Gold Coast, Nigeria, Sierra Leone and the Gambia in what has been called the first 'wave' of European expansion into West Africa.

The second stage involved the capture, settlement and expansion of

South Africa from the beginning of the nineteenth century (Cape of Good Hope) and of the further expansion of the South African colonies into the area known as Rhodesia and Nyasaland, which took place at the end of the nineteenth century. This was part of a greater plan devised by Cecil Rhodes, the British adventurer and empire-builder (who gave Rhodesia its name) to spread British power and influence from Cape Town to Cairo. Yet this power and influence presumed the settlement of British people in large tracts of Southern and Central Africa who would establish British culture in the heart of Africa for the benefit of British and African peoples.

The third stage brought East Africa into the Empire, a venture largely accomplished during the early part of the twentieth century. East Africa had no Cecil Rhodes to stimulate British settlement and it was in fact only in Kenya, with its rich Highlands and temperate climate that British immigrants settled. In Uganda and Tanganyika European settlement was much more sparse. In all three East African territories however, large numbers of Asians were transported as indentured labour for the construction of the railways or similar occupations on which native Africans were at that time insufficiently skilled to work; some of the East African tribes, for example, had not even been acquainted with the wheel before the arrival of the European at the beginning of the twentieth century.

In this chapter we discuss the cases of Ghana (formerly the Gold Coast) and Nigeria to illustrate the West African Commonwealth situation; for Central Africa we select the cases of (Southern) Rhodesia, Zambia (formerly Northern Rhodesia), and Malawi (formerly Nyasaland); for East Africa the three territories selected for discussion are Kenya, Uganda and Tanzania (formerly Tanganyika and Zanzibar). These territories are all Commonwealth states. However, there are a number of other states which are members of the Commonwealth as well which will not nevertheless be discussed here. These are the smaller West African states, Sierra Leone and the Gambia as well as the former so-called High Commission Territories, Lesotho (formerly Basutoland), Botswana (formerly Bechuanaland) and Swaziland in Southern Africa. South Africa itself has been considered above in Chapter 3.

West Africa has been part of British imperial history for longer than any other part of Africa, and British interest in West Africa has been evident for almost as long as British interest in India but British colonials never lived in West Africa over such a long period as they did in India.

Hence West Africa does not really enter British political consciousness until the present century.

Ghana

Ghana has become important in West African politics as the archetypal emergent Black African territory and its progress has been followed with great interest.[2] The present name of Ghana is derived from that given to an independent African kingdom in precolonial times, where a rich and powerful civilisation developed during the period approximating to the twelfth century in Europe. If we wish to impose a pattern on the political life of Ghana since British occupation, we might profitably see this in terms of five stages: colony, independent state, military rule (the first *coup*), resumption of civilian control, resumption of military rule (the second *coup*). We will consider this sequence in more detail.

The Gold Coast took its name from the obvious fact that the original interest of the Portuguese during the fifteenth century in exploring this coastal strip in West Africa lay in its rich trade in gold. In due course, this gave way to a far richer trade, the trade in human beings. The slave trade was formally abolished by Britain in the nineteenth century. The area was annexed by Britain in 1874 and in 1901 Britain further annexed the adjacent Ashanti kingdom as well as a territory to the north known as the Northern Territories. After the First World War Britain obtained part of the neighbouring area known as Togoland, previously a German colony and it too was administered as a part of the Gold Coast.

Gold Coast Africans were early participants in the movement towards a greater involvement in the administration of the territory and challenged the very right of the British to govern in the Gold Coast.[3] Particular mention might be made of John Mensah Sarbah, a Fanti from Cape Coast who was trained in the law and who criticised local government and taxation policies. Together with J. E. Casely Hayford he founded the Aborigines' Rights Protection Society in 1897; the key issue of their campaign was land. Later the Gold Coast found its strength under two leaders, J. B. Danquah and Kwame Nkrumah. Both challenged British authority, but Nkrumah's Ghanaian Convention Peoples Party was more successful, and under Nkrumah's resolute guidance led the Gold Coast to independence.

The state of Ghana was born on 5 March 1957, when the colony of the Gold Coast and the Trusteeship territory of Togoland became established as a Dominion. Ghana began its career with a number of advantages not always given to later colonies; it had a trained administrative framework of lawyers, doctors, and economists. Its treasury reserves amounted to US$560 million and its economy, though heavily dependent on cocoa production, was buoyant by any standards. Moreover, its leader, Kwame Nkrumah, appeared to be a man totally dedicated to his people and was regarded as the selfless embodiment of the new African spirit of independence and the harbinger of African decolonisation in the 'winds-of-change' era.

Nkrumah had, by 1962, become a ruthless dictator. He established a pattern soon to become typical of many African states both within and outside the Commonwealth. Ghana became a single-party state with absolute powers vested in Nkrumah as head of state, government and party, with the right to rule without parliament whenever he deemed this to be necessary. All criticism was punishable, imprisonment for an indefinite time without trial was commonplace. Imposed industrialisation and forced development of agriculture in state farms were both failures. As these failures became more apparent, so Nkrumah ignored them and turned not to their correction but to further acts of tyranny. His excesses produced, with all the inevitability of a Greek drama, a reaction or nemesis which led in 1966 to his removal. By 1965 it was clear that Ghana was on the point of economic collapse as foreign exchange reserves dropped to zero, cocoa prices fell and import credits eroded. Nkrumah, (now styled 'Osagyefo' or Redeemer) ordered numerous arrests of his own political party, the Convention People's party, and retreated to isolation, unaware of the long queues of disillusioned people who waited for the basic but scarce foodstuffs in fear and frustration.

In February 1966, while he visited Peking on a grandiose visit to bring peace to Vietnam, Nkrumah was removed by a remarkable *coup d'ĕtat* led by Colonel Joseph Ankrah. Ghana was now ruled by a National Liberation Council, the prototype for many subsequent military regimes. Nkrumah was given asylum in Guinea where he became (in association with President Sekou Touré of that country), a co-President. The military government announced, in a communiqué: 'The myth surrounding Kwame Nkrumah has been broken. . . . [He] ruled the country as if it were his private property. . . . [His] capricious handling of the country's economic affairs. . . . brought the country to the point of economic collapse.'[4]

Yet Nkrumah's economic problems were also those of the military regime. Cocoa production was below expectation and a relatively low production figure of 371,000 tons was reached in 1970. Ghana's debt remained close to US$1,000 million. The military government also encountered problems. Ankrah admitted receiving money from a private company and was succeeded by Colonel Akwasi Afrifa, author of the famous book on the *coup* which displaced Nkrumah.

The Constitution of the Second Republic of Ghana came into force on 22 August 1969 and ended with a bloodless coup on 13 January 1972. The restoration of civilian government in 1969 was widely welcomed, and although some people expressed caution, most were optimistic about the future. The optimists regarded it as evidence that Ghanaians had ended the acquiescence with military rule, a temporary phenomenon whose object was the purification of Ghanaian politics (in spite of the financial indiscretions of Ankrah himself). The President, now a figurehead in contradistinction to the autocratic rule of Nkrumah was the former Chief Justice Edward Askufo-Addo. The new prime minister, Nkrumah's rival, Kofi A. Busia, had long been in exile in Holland, where he had been established as a professor of sociology. The constitution of the second republic was written in the classical democratic style, complete with separation of powers, and checks and balances to ensure no further appearance of a new Nkrumah.

The *coup* of January 1972 once again deposed a civilian government, that of Kofi Busia, and a National Redemption Council (NRD) was established to administer the political affairs of Ghana. The presidential office was abolished, the National Assembly was dissolved, and all political parties were prohibited. Ghana was divided into nine military and administrative regions. The *coup,* which was a bloodless affair, was directed by Colonel I. K. Acheampong who accused the Busia administration of a total lack of resolution in controlling the problems of the economy, particularly as regards the exchange value of Ghana's currency and the state of the country's foreign reserves.

A question frequently asked by westerners who survey the many changes in African politics is: are these changes fundamental in the political direction of a country, in this case a Commonwealth African country, or are they no more than palace revolutions, or a game of political musical chairs, reshuffles involving no more than a replacement of figureheads? It is difficult to believe that *coups*, which take place in the capital and a few of the larger towns in any African state have much more than a marginal influence upon the lives of the people. Some indication of the state of the economy before and after a *coup* gives some indication of the truth or falsity of this notion. Ghana's economic situation, already unhealthy at the moment of Nkrumah's removal, deteriorated still further when the world price of cocoa fell during the later years of the 1960s. The disastrous downward move in the price of cocoa has been crucial in the development of post-independence Ghana. The resulting impact upon the economy is likely to have further and more specifically political repercussions. Politicians are expected to be able to solve such problems as those which beset Ghana; if they cannot they must expect to be called in question and possibly removed from office. Politics is frequently supposed to have therapeutic powers. In many Black African states such as Ghana the army acts as a curative or purgative force when politicians fail to produce results.

Nigeria

The modern state of Nigeria was the creation of British colonial policy, and the result of the efforts of a great colonial administrator, Lord Lugard. The very word 'Nigeria' was invented by Britain to describe the whole area. The three territories, or regions as they are normally called are in every sense disparate. The west is populated by an urbanised tribe, the Yorubas, with developed social, economic and political inclinations, but inclined to accept tradition and authority in their institutions. On the eastern side, the Ibos are renowned for their democracy, industry, vigour and a streak of stubborn determination which led them to secede from Nigeria in 1967. The northern region which is underdeveloped in comparison with the other two is peopled by the seminomadic theocratic Hausa. The northern region is regarded more as a part of the Sahara than as part of the coastal tropics. Nigeria therefore contains three major traditional political cultures which have always been a basic obstacle to national integration.

The exact population of Nigeria is something of an unknown factor because census-taking has often been a politically delicate matter. The size of each of the three regions has been a matter of controversy, involving questions of distribution of resources. However, the three regions (constituted since 1967 as twelve constituent states) contain over 60 million people. This makes Nigeria the most populous state in

Africa, containing about one-fifth of that continent's population. Nigeria is a federation, but the federation has been a century in the making. The colony and protectorate of Lagos was combined by stages with other annexed territories in the Niger valley creating in 1900 Northern and Southern Nigeria. In 1914 the 'colony and protectorate of Nigeria' was established, and in 1954 Nigeria became a federation under a Governor-General. Nigeria became independent in October 1960 and a republic in October 1963.

Somewhat similar to the case of Ghana, Nigeria has had a civilian stage followed by a military stage since independence. There have been two *coups* since 1966, and a civil war resulting in the secession of the Eastern region in 1967, which lasted until April 1968. We may therefore explore Nigeria's development under the following headings: colony, independent civilian rule, military rule, civil war and the postwar period.

From January 1914 Nigeria was defined as 'the colony and protectorate of Nigeria', under a Governor. In practice the three territories were administered differently, largely because of the vast differences between them. The Hausas of Zaria, the Bantu tribesmen of the Valley of the Benue and the Fantis of the Cape Coast were less closely allied with each other than were, for example, the Scandinavians of the Baltic and the peoples of Egypt or Bulgaria. One Nigerian leader, Chief Awolowo, stated just before independence three propositions within which the whole meaning of colonial rule must be understood:

1 that Nigeria is a British creation;
2 that Nigeria consists of a multiplicity of races who are as different from each other as the races in Europe;
3 that for forty-three years past, the British have striven to unite all these diverse peoples. . . . and to infuse in them a sense of common nationality.[5]

The British were sceptical as to whether a 'Nigerian nation' existed. Moreover, British colonial policy was based on indirect rule, devised by Sir Frederick Lugard later Lord Lugard (see p.32 above), a system which permitted local rulers, where these existed, to continue their particular mode of administration with British officials acting as non-involved 'overlords'. Nigerian development before independence was firmly fixed in regional categories which effectively became vertical pressure groupings on the national scene.[6]

The year 1960 was described as 'Africa's Year', during its course seventeen African territories gained independence.[7] Nigeria was the largest of these territories and the one on which hopes were set for successful democratic and federal independence. Cultural and ethnic differences however, were not to be submerged merely because Nigeria had obtained its political independence from Britain. There was a marked over-representation of Ibos and Easterners in positions of influence. At the federal level the regions of the north and east worked together but in the north itself where the Ibos occupied many positions of influence great bitterness developed because of the power of the Ibos in the government and economy of Northern Nigeria.

The government of the whole federation was directed from Lagos, the federal capital. The period of civilian rule, however, was short and characterised by intense bargaining as between the parties of the two southern groups, Yoruba and Ibo, in various combinations and the conservative North. When Nigeria was poised on the point of independence, a compromise northern candidate Sir Abubakar Tafewa Balewa emerged at the head of a coalition government. In 1964 elections were held which saw a clear collision between North and South which the coalition might have prevented.

Three years after independence, in 1963, Nigeria became a federal republic within the Commonwealth, but this was a formality which masked the grim significance of factional struggle between parties and regions. The difficulties were further exacerbated by corruption and ethnic conflict. The military *coup* which followed in 1966 therefore came with little surprise.

Nigeria's first successful *coup* took place on 15 January 1966 when a group of twenty-five officers removed Sir Abubakar Tafewa Balewa, the federal Minister of Finance Chief Festus Okatie-Eboh, the prime minister of the Western region Chief S. L. Akintola, the prime minister of the Northern region Sir Ahmadu Bello, and Lieut-Col. Jack Pam, the Adjutant-General of the Army. The overwhelming majority of the senior military officers killed were Northerners. Within two days Major-General Johnson Aguiyi-Ironsi, the head of the army, had assumed supreme power.

Ironsi suspended the constitution and abolished all political parties and associations based on tribes. The three 'regions' were redesignated as 'provinces'. The army set up a supreme military council which effectively became the Nigerian government. Ironsi's rule lasted only six months; in July 1966 he was overthrown in an internal military *coup* which resulted in the installation of Yakubu Gowon as a compromise candidate for military leadership. Gowon reinstated the federal form of government on military lines turning the Nigerian provinces once more into regions with Lagos as capital.

Further experiments took place with the delicate question of federal organisation in mind. On 27 May 1967 the Federal Republic was divided yet again into twelve states, in order to create an administrative structure designed as part of General Gowon's plans of underplaying the old regions so that, as he later put it, 'all energies will now be bent to the task of reintegration and reconciliation'.

The Eastern region was the Ibo area whose people were an energetic and industrious community. The Ibos resented the fact that Northerners (who constituted a state of over 32 million people) controlled Nigeria's central government. They saw the federation as a clamp on their energies and one moreover designed to hold them in numerical subordination to the states less developed group. On 30 May 1967 Lieut-Col. Ojukwu, Military Governor of the Eastern region, announced the creation of a new Ibo state, to be called Biafra, and the immediate secession of the East from the Federal Republic of Nigeria. What followed was one of the unhappiest phases in modern African political history.[8] As many as 30,000 Ibos in the north were massacred and many more fled to their homeland in the east from the various parts of Nigeria where they had settled. Initially Ojukwu's army advanced into the Mid-West area, but the Biafran victory was only temporary. By the end of 1967 the federal army had retaken the territory and had proceeded to invade Biafra, gradually occupying the whole of the Ibo homeland. The Biafrans fought tenaciously, assisted by France and Portugal; Britain and the Russians helped the federal side. A number of Commonwealth states also supported Biafra. However, the rebellion collapsed early in 1970, Colonel Philip Effiong surrendered to the federal army and Ojukwu went into exile in Guinea.

Nigeria's current political difficulties as always, whether or not the army is in control, derive from a need to preserve some sort of tribal balance in the federation. There are of course other divisions: according to earlier census figures Nigeria has over 26 million Muslims, and about 20 million Christians (Catholics and Protestants); and there are over 10 million followers of other religions. Economic resources are also a source of friction, particularly as Nigeria's oil production rose 100 per cent between 1969 and 1971, and is now over one million barrels per day. Civilian rule is not envisaged before 1976 (and perhaps not even then) when Nigeria will have been under military rule for over ten of its sixteen years of independence. Perhaps more accurately, Nigeria may be said to have forged an alliance between civilian and military bureaucracies.

Nigeria has tried 'free-fight democracy' to use Sukarno's term for western democracy, but has been unable to utilise it. The rule of the military has appeared to be the only solution to chronic political indiscipline, but there are many who hope that the more democratically acceptable norms of the West can be re-established.

South Africa

The place of South Africa in any account of Commonwealth and Empire history is of paramount importance and has been discussed in Chapter 3. Strictly speaking, South Africa is no longer a part of the Commonwealth and consequently has to be excluded from any account of the role of the Commonwealth in African countries. The Cape Province was, however, the springboard for the penetration of the southern part of the continent and from the Cape British influence was extended northwards towards what today are Lesotho, Botswana, Swaziland and Rhodesia.

The departure of South Africa from the Commonwealth in 1961 did not end British interest, trade and investment in that country (now the Republic of South Africa), and even today Britain takes over one-third of South Africa's exports (although South Africa takes only 4 per cent of British exports). The size of this trade is significant but so too is Britain's trade with what is called Black Africa. In 1971 Nigeria became Britain's thirteenth most important export customer and British trade with Black Africa is big enough to give African Commonwealth states a voice in the Commonwealth's most important decisions.

Rhodesia

Rhodesia is a small landlocked state in Central Africa which one might have expected to have been largely ignored by history. In fact, the problem of Rhodesia has rarely been far from the conscience or even consciousness of the Commonwealth for the very simple reason that after the withdrawal of South Africa, Rhodesia became the only white supremacist state in the whole of Commonwealth Africa. After 1965 Rhodesia became the most difficult Commonwealth issue, and one which threatened, at some stages, to cause serious disruption, if not the actual termination of the Commonwealth itself. It is therefore of some importance to explore the situation in some detail to understand the present predicament.

Political development since the foundation of the Rhodesias in 1898 can be seen as occurring in four stages: colonial rule up to 1923, responsible government 1923 to 1953, the period of federal government 1953 to 1963, and finally, Rhodesia since independence, 1965.

After the Treaty of Berlin, 1885, the Matabele kingdom of Lobengula (virtually co-extensive with present Rhodesia) was accepted by the European powers as being firmly in the British sphere of influence. In 1898 Lobengula agreed to make a concession of mineral rights to the British and in the following year the British South Africa Company was set up to exploit the land. Cecil Rhodes, who master-minded the scheme to develop the area, was born in 1853, the son of a clergyman; he went to South Africa on medical advice. He soon showed an aptitude amounting almost to genius for business and finance, and in some ways he made possible the development of the mineral riches of South Africa. At Kimberley he devoted his energies to building up the diamond industry associated with the De Beers group.

By 1881 Rhodes had amassed a fortune which produced an income amounting to about £1 million a year. He proposed to use it 'to paint the heart of Africa British red without cost to the British imperial exchequer'. The British government fully approved of the latter proposition but not wholly of the first; Rhodes was authorised to rule and administer lands lying between the Limpopo and Zambesi rivers. This project naturally encompassed the Northern Rhodesian area which was known to possess valuable mineral resources, but the scale of the project involved countries and governments and far exceeded the area of business operations. Rhodes therefore turned from economics to politics with little difficulty, becoming prime minister of Cape Colony with the dual object of furthering British expansion to the north and of preventing the Boers (led by Paul Kruger) from cutting off the route north from the Cape.

Accomplishment of these plans was not easy. Boers, Germans and Portuguese had designs on the lands which Rhodes saw to be indispensable to further British expansion. The so-called 'Missionaries' Road' developed by Livingstone and Moffat was described by Rhodes as the Suez Canal to the North. Bechuanaland was absorbed, not by South

Africa but by Whitehall direct. To the north again was Matabeleland, to which Rhodes had now been given rights, the land of the Matabele which was itself the route both to the geographical heart of Africa as well as to the region's valuable mineral deposits. These lands were eventually to be named after Rhodes, as Northern and Southern Rhodesia.

Rhodes's political ideas are important in themselves and provide enlightenment towards an understanding of subsequent Rhodesian political history. He expressed his views on political rights in a famous speech at Kimberley in 1898:

> My motto is equal rights for all civilised men south of the Zambesi. What is a civilised man? A man whether white or black who has sufficient education to write his name has some property and works, in fact is not a loafer.

This speech has had the effect of crystallising thinking on Rhodesia's constitutional and political problems ever since. All the various constitutional proposals which have been suggested since 1898 have in a sense been affected by Rhodes's statement. We may perhaps consider for a moment how they may be interpreted.

Originally Rhodes believed that it was necessary to include the Boers in South Africa in a political scheme which would create a unified Southern African state under British leadership. When he thought of 'race' he thought of the difference between Dutch (or Boers) and English. He never really envisaged that Africans or even people of mixed race (coloureds) were to be included in the scheme. Consequently it would be wrong to interpret his statement as having a liberal connotation; however, as it stands it suggests that if education and property barriers can be overcome then there are no further obstacles to the 'equal rights' of which he spoke.

Nearly all subsequent discussion in Rhodesia regarding constitutional development has hinged on the question of the mechanism by which the franchise is to be granted to a larger electorate. Such a view was at variance with that expressed by the Boers in South Africa, who would never accept equality with Africans. However, at the end of the nineteenth century, the great African Matabele chief, Lobengula was inclined to take a cynical view of the activities of the British Empire in his kingdom. He saw the British, as he put it, in the form of a chameleon, with himself as a fly, awaiting the inevitable fate, that of being swallowed up by the predator.

The notion of a merger between the Union of South Africa and Rhodesia was widely canvassed as a sensible move for the consolidation of Southern Africa and so to create a fifth province of South Africa. Such a proposal appeared on the surface to be a sensible geopolitical tidying up operation, as a separate Southern Rhodesia outside the Union would always lose the benefits of union. A referendum on the subject produced a vote in favour of separate responsible government for Rhodesia by a narrow majority:

For a separate Rhodesian responsible government	8,774
For joining the Union of South Africa	5,989

In 1923 therefore we saw the emergence in Rhodesia of a responsible government yet with a dependent status and certain limitations regarding the rights of Africans. Rhodesia was in effect a dominion on the lines of Australia, New Zealand and Canada, but with ultimate dependence on the British Crown. In fact the British government never exercised its powers. Hence the Rhodesian constitution was always somewhat unusual and its relationship to South Africa always unexplained. By 1960 Rhodesia's white population was about one-third South African born, one-third British born and one-third Rhodesian born.

British plans in the late 1940s and early 1950s for constitutional change throughout the Commonwealth included a plan to amalgamate Southern and Northern Rhodesia with Nyasaland. A move in this direction had already been made when in 1939 a Rhodesian Court of Appeal was set up for the three territories. At the same time the British government favoured the establishment of a large state in Central Africa based on the principle of partnership between the races. African nationalists attacked the whole proposal because they feared that it would imply the effective granting of power to the whites in the federation.

A shortlived Central African Federation was formed in 1953. It lasted, in Sir Roy Welensky's words, for 4,000 days (during part of which time Welensky, a former Northern Rhodesian politician was prime minister), and foundered on the question of African hostility and growing British doubts as to its effectiveness. In May 1963 the British government announced its decision to dissolve the Federation which came to its end on 31 December the same year. Nyasaland became Malawi in July 1964, and Northern Rhodesia was established as Zambia in October 1964, after ten months of internal self-government.

Southern Rhodesia henceforward became designated simply as Rhodesia, the only area remaining as part of the legacy of Rhodes. An 'independence' constitution was devised in 1961 and approved by 42,000 voters, with 21,846 opponents. This constitution fell short of full independence and instituted two categories of voters, depending upon education and property tests – a variation of Rhodes's 'equal rights for all civilised men', because it set out a method by which 'civilisation' could be achieved and the vote extended to Africans. If the system had been allowed to work from 1961 an African majority would have been feasible some time after 1980.

Yet in 1962, all hope that African majority rule would be achieved so simply – 'unimpeded progress towards majority rule' was its usual expression – was lost, when a new victorious party won the election of 1962. The Rhodesian Front did not intend that Government would fall into the hands of Africans, or as the Front put it, it would keep 'government in responsible hands'. In 1965 the Rhodesian Prime Minister, Ian Smith, declared Rhodesia to be independent of any control by the British Government; it took another five years for this to be translated into a severance of the ties with the British Queen.

Rhodesia's self-declared unilateral declaration of independence (commonly UDI) presented the Commonwealth with its greatest challenge.[9] The Tanganyikan Minister of External Affairs, Oscar Kambona, had already said in 1963 that if Britain did not grant majority rule in Southern Rhodesia, 'the entire African states membership of the Commonwealth would have to be considered'. Tanzania, Zambia and Ghana threatened to leave the Commonwealth if Britain, having failed to grant majority rule in Rhodesia, did not end the rebellion by force, but none of these countries did leave because in fact the Commonwealth was clearly of greater importance to Africa than to Britain. In December 1965 Ghana and Tanzania both broke off diplomatic relations with Britain, but did not withdraw from the Commonwealth. In February 1966 Nkrumah was overthrown by military *coup*, yet, with great disregard for diplomatic and constitutional niceties, the new regime asked for British diplomatic recognition (which it obtained), even though it had no diplomatic relations with Britain. Despite the anger of Commonwealth states, the Rhodesian impasse continued. Britain failed to solve it by direct discussions between Ian Smith and Harold Wilson, the British prime minister, on two warships, the '*Tiger*' and the '*Fearless*' in 1966 and 1968 respectively, and the matter was referred to the United Nations Security Council, which imposed mandatory sanctions on Rhodesia.[10]

Many experts predicted that Rhodesia could not survive the enormous pressure of international boycott.[11] However, sanctions were difficult to enforce because a number of countries continued to trade with Rhodesia, while South Africa and Portugal maintained policies of unbroken normal trade. Goods from West Germany, France, Holland, Japan, Sweden and even Britain were easily obtainable in Salisbury and Bulawayo. Rhodesia obtained oil from Portuguese East Africa and exported minerals to pay for her imports. Some tobacco was successfully exported but the Government heavily subsidised Rhodesian farmers. By 1973 Rhodesian trade was, despite sanctions, operating successfully at pre-UDI figures, and in that year wages rose by 5 per cent for Africans and 8 per cent for whites.

In 1971 the British Conservative Government negotiated an agreement with the Rhodesians but a large 'no' verdict was obtained when these proposals were put to Africans by a British Commission under Lord Pearce. The two governments had agreed on settlement terms, but the difficulty was that the African population did not trust the Rhodesian government to implement those terms, which in any case were unacceptable to most Africans. During 1972 and 1973 guerrilla activity increased and it was clear that no government with a majority of white Rhodesians could successfully attract even moderate African support such as the African National Council. The position obtaining in 1973 was put succinctly by *The Times* in connection with the trial of a journalist for the publication of security information:

> Rhodesia lives in a world of its own. Its Government's press relations are bad because its relations with the world are bad, and its relations with the world are bad because its relations with the majority of its own people are bad,

and it concluded that the Rhodesian Government felt 'insecure and morally beleaguered' (3 May 1973).

Both Rhodesia and Ian Smith have shown great capacity for political survival during the period from 1965 to 1975. They have successfully defeated all opponents and confounded all the prophets who have either spoken or acted against the regime. Yet this survival has not solved any problems nor has it given any clear future policy for a country in which Whites are out-numbered by twenty-two to one. Time is not on the side of the White Rhodesians.

Zambia

Between 1851 and 1873 the great Scottish explorer David Livingstone undertook wide and deep penetrations into Central Africa from the Indian Ocean to the Victoria Falls, in the area of the Zambesi river and out to the Atlantic on the other side. His reports produced an enormous interest in England where Africa was regarded as being as remote as the moon is today. In 1891 the British South Africa Company, which was developing local copper finds came to administer the territory which was to be known as Northern Rhodesia, and officially so designated from 1911. In 1924 the office of Governor and an executive council were created and the British South Africa Company handed over its powers to the Crown.

Northern Rhodesia proved to be rich in copper, the extensive discovery of which led, between 1930 and 1944, to a 'copper rush' during which European settlement increased tenfold.[12] Northern Rhodesia was incorporated into the Federation in 1953 which terminated on 31 December 1963; on that date Zambia was formed as an independent African state. In 1972 it was announced that Zambia would become a single-party state.

Zambia came into existence with two major parties reflecting the principal tribal and regional rivalries: the Lozis of Barotseland and the Bemba of the North. Rivalry between the two tribal groups is of comparatively recent origin. The vehicle for independence was the United National Independence Party (UNIP) led by Kenneth Kaunda; the opposition African National Congress was led by Harry Nkumbula. Nkumbula advocated policies radically different from those of Mr Kaunda, including a softer attitude towards South Africa and Rhodesia. Events continued to move towards a single-party system and to a politicisation of the civil service. 'When I appoint a civil servant,' said Kaunda in 1966, 'it will be because he is loyal to UNIP.' Nkumbula was imprisoned and the ANC gradually lost its strength to combat the all-powerful UNIP. It was perhaps inevitable therefore that the ANC should become outlawed, with Kaunda's position further entrenched. The Government obtained powers after a referendum in June 1969 to alter any section of the Constitution by a two-thirds majority. In the same year, the European Chief Justice (a Zambian citizen and founder-member of UNIP), together with two other European judges, retired after 'difficulties' with the President over a verdict involving illegal entry into Zambia by two Portuguese soldiers.

President Kaunda is one of the Commonwealth African leaders to have made interesting incursions into what might broadly be called 'political philosophy'. He has been strongly influenced theoretically by Gandhi's 'philosophy' of non-violence. In office, however, he has demonstrated a passionate desire to repress the so-called Lumpa Church led by its so-called prophetess of the Church, Alice Lenshina, whose capture, 'dead or alive' he advocated. He stated to Parliament in Lusaka: 'My government will spare no efforts to bring them [the Lumpa-ites] down as quickly as possible. Even if it means other people calling me savage then I am going to be one.'

Kaunda also strongly advocated the use of force against Rhodesia describing Britain as a 'humbled toothless bulldog' when she refused to send paratroops to safeguard the Kariba Dam. However, he did refrain from taking Zambia out of the Commonwealth, and even accepted British military assistance and training for the Zambian army. In wrestling with his conscience Kaunda demonstrated that he was interested in making the attempt to discover some form of principles of political legitimacy. Dr. Banda on the other hand has not been worried by questions of legitimacy, but simply rules. Kaunda has returned to his penchant for political moralising with the formulation of a Gandhian doctrine known as 'humanism'. Humanism envisages a vague combination of attributes, including 'participatory democracy', control by UNIP and rural development.

In international affairs, Zambia found itself under great pressures. The country contains a quarter of the world's known exploitable copper, but there are no means of transporting the ore to the sea other than by rail either through Rhodesia or across Portuguese territory. Kaunda wished to escape from this unwelcome dependence and agreed to accept a Chinese loan of about US$336 million to build a 1,000 mile railway outlet from the copper belt area to Dar-es-Salaam in Tanzania. This railway would, after 1975, annually transport Zambia's 750,000 tons of copper to the sea.

Kaunda's Zambia chose to merge its destinities with those of the north rather than with Rhodesia and the white southern part of Africa. When Rhodesia unilaterally declared independence Kaunda continually deplored British inaction and one of his ministers expressed his 'utter disgust with the way the Wilson Government has handled the rebellion in Rhodesia by resorting to ineffective means instead of bringing down the rebellion by force'. After the Smith-Wilson talks on HMS *Fearless* in October 1968, Kaunda described the new proposals as 'a despicable surrender to racialism'.

The activities of guerrilla forces in the Zambesi Valley produced the greatest dissension between the two states of Zambia and Rhodesia, and in January 1973, Rhodesia closed its border with Zambia as a reprisal for the latter's alleged support for the guerrillas (and numbered amongst the dead were South African 'policemen'). The Zambians also experienced a deterioration in relations with Portugal and Malawi over border incidents. Zambia has adopted unorthodox positions from time to time on the status of Commonwealth African states, and recognised Biafra (as did Tanzania) when that 'state' broke away from the Nigerian federation. Kaunda also held that, even after his deposition, Nkrumah was still the President of Ghana, and argued that African military governments, with few exceptions, were generally unwelcome. Zambia resolutely set her face to the north.

Malawi

Malawi is the presentday independent version of the protectorate of Nyasaland, a small narrow area in Central Africa first visited in 1859 by David Livingstone, the Scottish missionary and explorer, principally to put an end to the slave trade. The land round Lake Nyasa (now Lake Malawi) gradually came under British control as a protectorate in 1891. Over half a century later, in 1953, Nyasaland was joined to the Central African Federation despite a stronger opposition among the Nyasa people, than was experienced in Northern Rhodesia. Malawi's President, Dr Hastings Banda, was called back to Nyasaland in 1958 to lead the struggle conducted by young politicians against the Central African Federation. His vigorous and successful campaign in this cause gained him immense popularity and unquestioned authority, although he spent a period of time in prison charged with plotting the deaths of white officials. In 1960 Britain granted a constitution to Nyasaland assuring an African majority in the legislative council and in 1963 Malawi gained independence. In September 1964 Banda summarily dismissed three of his ministers (whom he accused of conspiring to accept a bribe of £18m in return for Malawi's recognition of Peking), and Henry Chipembere, the leader of the revolt was forced into exile. Banda quickly consolidated his power by establishing Malawi as a republic, with himself as life president and the country as a single-party state.

Today, Malawi's political system is highly personalised and the President's control over the Malawi Congress Party is complete. Opposition to the regime has been virtually eliminated. President Banda has rejected both apartheid and what he sees as irrational outbursts on the part of certain Black states in their animosity towards South African economic resources and power. In October 1967 he entered into diplomatic relations with Pretoria. Malawi is not exactly a captive nation but because she is landlocked and in close proximity to white southern Africa, she is vulnerable to their pressures and influences, and her African population is to a large extent employed in neighbouring countries, including Rhodesia, (where there are 200,000), in South Africa (80,000), Zambia (20,000) and Tanzania (15,000). Malawi depends partly on the remittances of these expatriate workers, who help to sustain the economy. British aid has been the principal support of the budget, helping to bridge the trade deficit with annual subventions of between £1m to £2m. Malawi's economic prospects have greatly improved, however, as bauxite deposits have been developed, while South African investment and aid have been used to promote the growth of cash crops. The complications of Rhodesian UDI have led to the development of new trading routes.

Given Dr Banda's virtual total control and his 'good neighbour policies' with regard to South Africa, Mozambique and Rhodesia, Malawi's relations with her neighbours has been described as 'rather lonely'. Africans in Rhodesia advised by Dr Banda that there were 'many ways of killing a cat', which implied that they could become successful by means other than by force. Quite clearly Banda's acceptance of South African material support, in the form of technical aid and financial assistance for special projects, was totally unacceptable to his neighbours in Black Africa, In 1969 Malawi refused to join in a manifesto criticising white neighbours to the south, thus becoming out of step with the Organisation of African Unity. Relations between Malawi and Tanzania deteriorated to an exceedingly low level. Quite early on, in October 1965, President Julius Nyerere of Tanzania argued that Malawi could not properly take its place on the African Liberation Committee not only because of the acceptance of South Africa's race policies, but also because of the rights claimed in respect of the international boundary between the two countries. Malawi's relations with Zambia have also been unhappy under the Banda administration, partly because of the incompatibility with regard to South Africa, but also because many Zambians and Malawians are ethnically similar.

It is a matter of some debate whether Malawi's political style is likely to survive Banda's eventual demise. Indeed, it may be argued that all Malawi's political thinking is attributable to one man. Banda-ism is most frequently associated with realism and is in the best traditions of the *realpolitik* of Cavour and Bismarck. 'I would do a deal with the devil,' said Dr Banda, 'if it were for the good of Malawi.' Several High Court judges schooled in the niceties of constitutional procedure, resigned in 1969, as Banda did not hesitate to have eight men executed in June 1968 for their part in an attempted assassination.

Hastings Banda often reminds the observer of Commonwealth affairs of the style and methods of Lee Kuan Yew in Singapore; both, for example, were hostile to long hair, miniskirts and the 'permissive' society. And there is the same general determination to sustain an apparently non-viable economic state. While Malawi has continued to depend on external capital for its survival, Singapore has produced a dynamic economy in South-east Asia, but, despite the great economic differences, there has been a certain similarity in the political style of the two leaders, notably different, for example, from that of Nyerere and Kaunda.

East Africa

The British came to East Africa in the wake of the proposed partition of Africa in the 1880s. A convention amongst the powers making claims to various parts of Africa was that it was necessary to obtain 'treaties' from African chiefs. The Imperial British East Africa Company for example provided its agents with blank forms on which simple 'treaties' could be drawn up. European occupation of Africa was an imposition of an alien culture upon a continent innocent of industrialisation, social change and technology of any sort. British interest in East Africa was initially keenest in the territory of Uganda.

Uganda

Uganda is today the name of a landlocked African state – a name which has been the object of some confusion. On arrival in the southern part of presentday Uganda, British explorers believed the term 'Uganda' to apply to a much larger area, extending to the borders of the Sudan. Uganda became a British protectorate, and by about 1914 consisted of a number of African groupings, tribes and kingdoms, from the Bantu of the south and west to the Nilotic tribes of the north. Uganda was a classic case of a territory arbitrarily created out of several different peoples without reference to ethnic considerations.

The Baganda, the people of the southern province of Buganda, enjoyed a position of high esteem with the British, partly because they were quick, energetic and receptive, partly because they appeared to have an established monarchy which produced a certain fascination for some British officials. In due course the Kabaka came mistakenly to be seen as a form of constitutional monarch on lines familiar to the home pattern. In 1900 an agreement between the British government and Buganda offered the latter limited sovereign rights, including the due acceptance of the place of the Kabaka and 'parliament' (lukiko), and consequently the Baganda came to see themselves as equals with the British in governing Buganda.[13]

The other three provinces of Uganda, the West (Toro), the East (Bunyoro) and the North (Acholi-Lango) made up the component parts of the protectorate as 'a series of mutually exclusive African governments responsible only to the British protectorate authority at the apex'.[14] There were strong pulls towards the districts. The early formation of a Ugandan nationalism became well-nigh impossible and indeed, as one local politician put it, Uganda's political life-style was a 'parochial affair'.[15]

Unlike Kenya, Uganda never experienced large-scale European settlement for a variety of reasons including government reluctance as well as the great distance of Uganda from the sea. However, during the colonial period hundreds of Indians were recruited to work on the Mombasa-Kampala railway, on the grounds that Africans were too 'primitive' to perform the tasks involved. The Indians stayed and prospered as merchants, eventually controlling the entire commercial structure not only in Uganda but in many other East and Central African states. Throughout the half-century 1900-50 the paramount constitutional issue in Uganda was that of Buganda separatism, in which the Kabaka was often seen as a focal point of Buganda (rather than Uganda) nationalism. Sir Andrew Cohen, governor of Uganda in the 1950s was a centraliser who saw the Kabaka, Mutesa, as a threat to plans to reduce separatism and so to create a unitary state. Mutesa was deported but the problem was exacerbated rather than solved.

The development of cash crops in Uganda was of great importance. Cotton production, for example, produced a mere £1,000 in 1905-06, but by 1914-15 had increased in value to £369,000. Yet European farming in Kenya produced a totally different agricultural pattern from peasant cultivation in Uganda. In the former country agriculture developed a much greater share of the gross national product than in the latter.

In October 1962 Uganda gained independence. A form of federal structure was suggested in which the Baganda kept their lukiko or parliament-type assembly, from which it chose representatives to sit in the national legislature. At the same time Buganda enjoyed a degree of local autonomy within the Uganda federation. Naturally the other parts of Uganda, Toro, Bungoro, Ankole and Busoga asked for similar concessions and even where this was much less directly applicable such as Acholi and Lango. The federation was dominated by Buganda interests. At Makerere University College over half of the students were Baganda, the schools of the Baganda provided the feeding process for higher education. Buganda was the area of the sophisticated economy. As one writer put it, while other Ugandans needed money to pay their poll tax, the Baganda perceived that money would also buy 'refrigerators, motor-cars and dinner jackets'.[16] Independence increased cultural and ethnic friction because the minority groups greatly feared that after the departure of the British their position would worsen.

In purely party political terms there were many complications. The Kabaka Yekka (Kabaka only party) symbolised Baganda mass aspirations. Benedict Kiwanuka, a Catholic Muganda commoner, became Uganda's first prime minister but, given the complexities of the political situation he could not long survive. That he was a Catholic unsettled Buganda's Protestants, and at the same time he appeared to Buganda loyalists to occupy a political position superior to that of his King.

Whatever were Buganda's internal difficulties they were of course only part of a wider question of Ugandan nationalism. Paradoxically it was Milton Obote, a Lango leader and a northerner, who resolved some of the difficulties by his astute political activities. Obote widened his support in Uganda by merging the Uganda National Congress (UNC), the nearest approach to a national party, with the Uganda People's Congress (UPC). Subsequently he constructed a coalition government which included the Kabaka Yekka, despite the Buganda exclusivism of the latter. This uneasy situation lasted until 1966 when Obote arrested several Kabaka Yekka members in his Cabinet, and deported the Kabaka, this time permanently. Uganda was given a unitary constitution, and Obote had finally accomplished by force of arms what the British had not been able to accomplish by negotiation.

President Obote was removed from office by the army *coup* during a Commonwealth 'occasion'. In January 1971 a lively Commonwealth Prime Ministers' Conference was held at Singapore. Most of the time was spent in criticism of Great Britain's inability to terminate the Rhodesian rebellion, an attack largely led by Obote, but he was unable to return to Uganda and went into exile in Tanzania.

The first speech on Radio Uganda after the *coup* of 25 January 1971 included eighteen reasons for the army takeover. These included detention without trial, corruption and unwarranted claims to having established social democracy in the country. The leader of the *coup* was General Amin, a long-serving soldier from the West Nile area of Uganda, and an unlikely head of state. He had no more than two years of primary education, a very inadequate command of English and a previous accusation of corruption and gold smuggling. However, he was to prove to be a bold tactical politician; in 1972 he expelled the unpopular non-citizen Asians who for so long had been the merchant class in Uganda, and nationalised British businesses. Both these moves were highly risky, but the effect was to create mass support making Amin a national leader. Added to this he controlled the army, in spite of its indiscipline during the removal of the Asians. The Chief Justice (Mr Kiwanuka, the former Prime Minister) and the Vice-Chancellor of Makerere University were shot and large numbers of officials and politicians 'disappeared'. Many missionaries were expelled. The British Foreign and Commonwealth Secretary, Sir Alec Douglas-Home told the House of Commons in December 1972 that President Amin's actions were 'outrageous by any standards of civilised behaviour and certainly incompatible with the behaviour expected within the Commonwealth partnership'. All aid money was stopped and Britain made arrangements to take in the deported Asians. The International Commission of Jurists alleged that the Ugandan authorities undertook the systematic killing of the President's political opponents. There is no doubt that Amin's Uganda was a state 'unhinged', as the erratic President moved forward in unpredictable and embarrassing ways.

Kenya

Kenya has been independent since December 1963 and has been a republic since December 1964. The country has experienced rapid and traumatic experiences in a period of little more than half a century since the first European entered Kenya. Effective British occupation of Kenya dates back to the 1890s, and in 1895 a protectorate was declared, a year after that over Uganda (Buganda). There was a famous cartoon in *Punch* showing how the liquidated British East Africa Company deposited a small black baby labelled 'Uganda' on the doorstep of Mr Gladstone, the prime minister, at No. 10, Downing Street. Gladstone contemplated his new acquisition with a total absence of relish. If the acquisition of Uganda displeased him that of Kenya pleased him even less; Uganda was in fact considered a more desirable proposition. Originally Kenya consisted of a colony and a barren strip belonging to the Sultan of Zanzibar; it was not until 1920 that 'greater Kenya' became a Crown colony.

However, the important decision was taken to build a railway from Mombasa on the coast to Uganda, using labour imported from India. From an engineering point of view the railway was a remarkable achievement. It began at sea level, climbed to 7,000 feet then dropped into the Great Rift Valley. From the Valley, the railway climbed 8,500 feet before it eventually arrived at the shores of Lake Victoria, 5,000 feet above sea level. It effectively opened up East Africa, provided access to the White Nile and above all, began the experiment of the European Highlands. The cost of £5.5 million was borne by British taxpayers. Kenya's temperate climate and agricultural potential held a great attraction for white settlement and Kenya became the only East African territory in which large-scale white settlement developed. Whites came to settle from 1902 in lands considered either vacant or 'belonging' to nomadic Masai hunters. Other Africans were given lands or reserves in which it was hoped they would live in peace.

The pioneer of white settlement was Lord Delamere, who showed Kenya's potential wealth by harvesting twenty bushels an acre on his plots at a time when Canada could produce only twelve. Kenya attracted many whites – 'impecunious adventurers seeking a new stake in life, land-poor gentry from Britain, retired soldiers on pension and Boers dissatisfied with conditions in South Africa'. Hopefully the British government envisaged the growth of a 'sturdy Anglo-Saxon yeomanry breathing life into a rich but unexploited land', but in fact Kenya was always a problem for the Colonial Office, the object of countless demands and pressures from settlers for a greater say in the country's affairs.[17] Constitutional commissions flourished on questions of land, law, franchise, the allocation of public monies to the various communities, and a grandiose plan to create a federal state consisting of the three territories of Kenya, Uganda and Tanganyika. Such a federal state was to be created in Central Africa in the 1950s with Southern Rhodesia playing the role which Kenya might have played.

The economic structure of the Kenyan economy is a subject worth pursuing. Between 1938 and 1952 exports increased in value seven times, based mainly on the production of white settler cash crops. Over these years the African contribution to national production was very small – 6 per cent in 1952, for example, compared with Uganda's 1951 figure of 63 per cent. At the same time, while the African population grew at an annual rate of 3 per cent, African real income from the market economy grew at the rate of only 1 per cent per annum. In large measure, the discontent of the population in Kenya under British rule developed from pressures of a growing population on land. In the 1950s, Kenya experienced the Mau Mau rebellion, which dragged on for six years.

The term 'Mau Mau', like the concept itself, was obscure in nature and origin. It was a Kikuyu movement, which employed methods of *traditional* fear and hostility towards the white settlers and fellow Kikuyu in order to advance the cause of *modern* African nationalism.[18] The Kikuyu argued that the white settled areas, known as the White Highlands, were taken from them by the whites. Others have argued that the Highlands were never Kikuyu territory except for a mere 105 acres which were paid for in cash. Yet the white farmers were manifestly more efficient and the value of the produce sold from the European farms was £10 million, compared with £3.5 million per annum from African farmers. At the same time the settlers contributed 70 per cent of the colony's total exports and paid more than twice as much as Africans in direct taxes. The emergency began in 1952 and involved minor civil disobedience, arson, destruction of property and a large number of killings. Most of those killed were Africans, and in fact Kikuyu. The emergency did force a greater recognition of African grievances, including the demand for the franchise which was granted in 1956 and paved the way for an eventual African government. Multiracial cooperation on a political level was unacceptable. In effect the writing was on the wall for those white settlers who sought permanent dominance on the Rhodesian model.

Kenyatta is one of the most important of all African nationalists. He was born in 1893 and began his career as a teacher. His political career began when he became General Secretary of the Kikuyu Central Association in 1928 and editor of its monthly journal. By his absence in Britain until 1946, Kenyatta managed to avoid intertribal squabbles, so that when he returned to Kenya in 1946 his chances of leadership were greatly enhanced. He produced a work of anthropology with the title '*Facing Mount Kenya*' (Heinemann, 1938), in which he tried to show that the Kikuyu really owned the White Highlands but happened to be absent when the Europeans arrived because of a Kikuyu land policy of shifting cultivation. In fact, Kikuyu society was already shaken by Western ideas and institutions, and when social practices such as female circumcision came under attack the tribe saw its whole culture, traditions and land claims at risk before the western onslaught.

Kenyatta was imprisoned as an alleged leader of Mau Mau but was subsequently released. He entered the Legislative Council as leader of the Kenya African National Union (KANU) with the combined support of Kikuyu and Luo tribes. His political astuteness was tested when the opposition Kenya African Democratic Union (KADU) was established in 1961 supported by a group of smaller tribal units. Kenyatta effected a cooperation of the two parties and led KANU to an overwhelming victory in May 1963. In December of the same year Kenya became independent with Kenyatta as first prime minister. Within a few months KADU voluntarily dissolved.

When Kenya became independent a manpower survey was conducted which showed that half of the posts requiring university or higher education were held by Europeans, but the demand for Kenyanisation has changed the position. Non-Kikuyus often complain that this effectively implies 'Kikuyu-isation' and they point to the disproportionate share of Kenya's resources in Kikuyu hands, from government posts to places at the university. For Africans generally, in the majority since 1963, the salient feature of independence has been an insistence on securing good jobs. Rapid Africanisation in the civil service led to the situation where by 1967, Kenyatta announced that 92 per cent of the civil service had been Africanised.[19] Employment in the modern sector and in the attractive towns provides the fortunate recipient with modern amenities, cars, television sets, modern plumbing and the Nairobi version of the *dolce vita.* But in independent Kenya there has existed a continuing debate over jobs and education, the keys to status and power. Africans have been taught to recognise the connection between skill and income and they have continued to struggle to possess these things, particularly in view of the fact of very high unemployment in Kenya.

The Kenya African National Union or KANU came into power as the party of independence in 1964. It was the descendant of an older grouping, the Kenya African Union, but has now come to be the single official party in the country. Yet within the party there are clear divisions which may perhaps be said to constitute mini-parties within the overall loose framework of the major party political grouping. Indeed the very diffuseness of KANU has caused some political scientists to speak of a 'no-party' state in Kenya. The government has run into problems and a good degree of faction fighting, for example between traditional Kikuyu (who set great store in the swearing of oaths) and modern Kikuyu thinking which spurned such unsophisticated practices while at the same time cautiously refusing their total abandonment. KANU was, as has been suggested, more than a typical African single party; it was a tool of political struggle at the top where faction fights were commonplace but are not reducible to a simple Kikuyu versus Luo conflict. Both Tom Mboya, a highly regarded trade union leader, and Odinga Odinga (leader of the Kenya People's Union) were Luo, and their rivalry in the mid-1960s was intense.

Broadly speaking, KADU represented those elements concerned about Kikuyu and Luo supremacy; it was headed by Ronald Ngala and Daniel Arap Moi. Although the 1961 election was won by KANU, this party refused to form a government while Kenyatta remained in detention. KADU's difficulties developed because of its minority status as well as on account of the overwhelming prestige of Kenyatta. However, in 1963 a new 'federal' solution emerged as KANU and KADU settled their differences and accepted Kenyatta as Kenya's first prime minister. In 1964, therefore, KADU dissolved itself and Kenya became a single-party state by agreement. At that stage Kenya had not yet fully formed the complex and sophisticated process of bargaining between large and small ethnic groupings.

The Kenya People's Union (KPU) was formed in 1966 by Odinga Odinga (a Luo), once a close supporter of Kenyatta. Odinga resigned from KANU on the grounds that it was 'capitalistic'. The Kenya government in turn attacked Odinga, accused him of 'subversion' and confiscated his passport. Finally, the constitution was amended to make it impossible for non-party candidates to stand for Parliament. President Kenyatta himself spoke of all KPU followers as 'snakes'. KPU members began to defect and in September 1968, twenty of them resigned and joined KANU, and despite the protests of students at Nairobi University College, Odinga was not allowed to speak there.

Power structures in Kenya are basically related to tribes and to a cluster of power groups within KANU. Those closest to the President clearly move closest to power. Younger Kikuyu are particularly important because they may turn their backs upon traditional clan conflicts, although it will be difficult to escape such conflicts in and around Nairobi itself. It is taken for granted that Kikuyu hegemony will continue, particularly since the assassination in 1969 of the talented Luo leader, Tom Mboya. Kenyatta has tried 'to balance the ticket' where appropriate by constituting his government on appeals to the various tribes, regions and districts, though it is fair to say that the Luo still feel themselves to be 'deprived'. At the same time, Kenyatta has been successful in his policy of bridge-building which allows for a political formula in which former Mau Mau leaders, former white settlers (but not Asians) and former black rivals can feel at home.

Kenya may accurately be described as a no-party state, using an electoral system borrowed from the British model. The central executive has become totally concentrated in Kenyatta whose charismatic powers have overshadowed party politics. What the constitution has been said to lack is a prime minister who can draw some of the power away not so much from the present President but from a less charismatic successor. Indeed the fear is that the entrenched powers of the Kikuyu tribe may become more deeply challenged after Kenyatta's death. Tribal balance is the key to successful politics and is a consideration which overrides factors like youth or ability. There have been alleged cases of corruption during the 1960s when certain ministers were accused of appropriating £1 million to their own use. Where tribal feelings run deep such practices are not entirely unexpected, and when Kenyatta is removed it would not be safe to imagine that Kenya's various tribes and races will find harmony easy to achieve.

Tanzania

Tanzania is a dual state consisting of territories formerly known as Tanganyika and Zanzibar. Tanganyika did not come into the British

Empire until as late as 1920. From 1885 to 1920 Tanganyika was known as German East Africa, but, as a result of Germany's defeat in World War I, most of German East Africa became a British mandate and and in 1946 became a trust territory under British administration.

As late as 1939 the mandate of Tanganyika was still largely untouched by westernisation and the various tribal groupings in the area were hardly to be seen as a Tanganyikan nation. Zanzibar was, on the other hand, the centre of an Arab slave-trading complex until, by the second half of the nineteenth century, the cultivation of cloves replaced the trade in slaves. Tanganyika obtained its independence in 1961, and Zanzibar was added in April 1964. Elections were held in October 1965, which joined representatives from Zanzibar into the Tanganyika African National Union (TANU).

TANU was established under the leadership of Julius Nyerere, a young African schoolmaster who had spent many years studying in Britain. Nyerere had been clearly under the influence of Scottish missionaries, who gave his political thinking an evangelical flavour. He has flirted with slightly mystical ideas and he has expounded a form of elementary 'socialism'. Given his religious background, Nyerere is unlikely to have espoused Marxist socialism with its indications of scientific thoroughness. Instead he has argued for an African socialism which stresses a fraternal notion of sharing; in view of Tanzania's fundamental poverty, he has had to stress a sharing of poverty as much as of wealth.

Great emphasis has been placed on the development of *ujamaa* villages in which self-help community development is fostered. There is a feeling in Tanzania that only the state, or the party, possess the authority and the resources to promote development. Nyerere has argued: 'I believe that no underdeveloped country can afford to be anything but 'socialist'. I believe, therefore, that we in Africa are bound to organise ourselves on a socialist pattern'. Rather more specifically he rejected European analyses of 'socialism' in Africa because of the clear difference in conditions; the term 'class' was, he argued, unknown in African languages.

Nyerere set out his policy objectives for development of Tanzania in 1968 with the well-known Arusha Declaration. The two major ideals of the declaration were a reliance on self-help and an idealistic form of egalitarianism. As regards the modern industrial sector of the economy, nationalisation was to be a basic policy, but it was far more difficult to mobilise the traditional peasantry. 'We are', said Nyerere, 'training for a socialist, self-respecting and self-reliant Tanzania.' The farms of a number of foreign farmers on the slopes of Kilimanjaro were nationalised, 'because it is our policy to create a socialist state' and those affected were not permitted to take their 'compensation' out of the country.

Tanzania is one of the poorest of all Commonwealth states and four-fifths of its population of about 13 million are to be found in the rural sector. At the same time the country laboured under a number of other disadvantages, such as the existence of as many as 120 different tribal groupings, poor communications, and an inappropriately sited capital (soon to be shifted from Dar-es-Salaam to Dodoma). Of all the difficulties facing Nyerere, however, none was more intractable than the question of Zanzibar.

In 1964, the Sultan of Zanzibar was deposed in a bloody *coup*. The Afro-Shirazi party established the People's Republic of Zanzibar until the unification of the Tanganyika mainland and Zanzibar as Tanzania. Zanzibar's policies have constantly been out of step with those of Nyerere on the mainland. The former Zanzibar vice-president Karume publicly denounced two of Nyerere's central policies; the non-racial policy and the Arusha Declaration. Karume stated that 'Tanzania is for black Africans and not others. If you in the mainland hide this fact from others we in the islands do not.'

The second challenge was directed towards the austere ethic of the Arusha Declaration, arguing that Zanzibar's leaders did not intend to forgo the pleasures of private property, directorships or the employment of servants. Zanzibari ministers were reported to hold considerable sums of money in foreign banks. Justice in Zanzibar has been singularly bizarre. Prisoners were released on the condition that they agreed to be shot if they repeated their crimes. Some Arabs were beaten to death after being made to dig their own graves first.[20]

Nyerere has always perceived Tanzania's membership of the Commonwealth in a very special way. He has clearly seen membership as implying some sort of minimum morality. Those members who cannot subscribe to this minimum morality should be removed, while those members who perceive implied threats to the morality through continued Commonwealth membership should withdraw.

With regard to Commonwealth dealings with Rhodesia and South Africa, Nyerere has been unequivocal. The Commonwealth should not only have no truck with the white-ruled states of Southern Africa; it should actively contemplate their 'liberation'. Nyerere even went so far as to decline an invitation to the independence celebrations of Swaziland on the grounds that this was not a 'true' independence. He broke off diplomatic relations with Britain over Rhodesian independence and threatened to leave the Commonwealth if British arms sales to South Africa were to exceed those laid down in the Simonstown Agreement. When the Uganda *coup* of 1971 took place, Nyerere reacted unsympathetically. 'How can I sit at a table with a killer?' he asked rhetorically on hearing of it. But by May 1972 he had become more reconciled to Amin and an uneasy peace prevailed.

Conclusion

Africa was the last great continent to be colonised and both colonisation and decolonisation has taken place there in less than a century. The conference in Berlin which 'legitimised' the partition of Africa took place in 1884, and most of the creations of the late nineteenth century had become 'states' by the 1960s. We are perhaps still too close to the colonial age for the quiet appraisal of the historian. Indeed the word 'colonialism' has become a curse on the lips of countless Africans and Asians.[21] In the 1950s the reputation of British colonialism had reached rock bottom. The historian, Richard Pares, writing in 1957 asked, almost despairingly: 'What answer are we to make to the revolt of three-quarters of the world against colonialism? Obviously we shall not say to the liberated peoples: "Come and stamp on us for a hundred years; then we shall be all square and you will feel better." '[22] With the passage of time, however, such sentiments, particularly with regard to Africa, may become less commonly expressed.

Modern African states appear to wish to preserve the Commonwealth. The former French colonies too still have a very strong attachment to France, thanks to the French talent for proselytising her culture as part of her *'mission civilisatrice'*. The Belgian experiment with colonisation was much less happy. The Congo (now Zaïre) was the private kingdom of King Leopold II until in 1908, under pressure from Britain and America, the Belgian government was forced to take over the territory which Leopold had governed so cruelly. Independence in 1960 was unplanned, unheeded and chaotic. A few days after independence there followed an army mutiny and an eventual army takeover. The Belgians have been the least successful decolonisers, and only the British have created that loose arrangement which we call the 'Commonwealth'.

All this may reflect what philosophers might recognise as British empiricism – the British way of doing things by precedent; Belgian platonism – the creation of a small class of elite Africans; and French cartesianism – decolonisation by definition from Paris. Yet only the Commonwealth remains as an institutional embodiment of the post-colonial age.

For many small countries of Commonwealth Africa the Commonwealth is important because it permits them to enjoy the advantages of big power status with none of the disadvantages. It would be wrong to see the Commonwealth in Africa either as a coherent purposeful force or as a meaningless menace. It is likely to survive for some time longer. Its survival in Africa depends on an acceptance of the principles of peaceful coexistence. Many people thought that it would not last after Rhodesian UDI. However, somewhat unexpectedly, the Commonwealth in Africa still survives after ten years of self-declared independence on the part of Ian Smith in Rhodesia. By 1974 it appeared to be accepted that Britain had little or no power over events in Africa, including those in her rebellious colony. Rhodesia's internal security moreover appeared to be increasingly endangered by guerrilla incursions, yet, barring some unforeseen contingencies, Rhodesia too appeared to be likely to survive for an indeterminate period longer.

Black Commonwealth Africa was confronted with many difficult problems. In West Africa, military influence flourished as well as regionalism; in East Africa the erratic behaviour of Uganda's President led to great hardship and eviction for Asian citizens in East Africa. In Central Africa, Zambia felt herself threatened by 'enemies' in the White South. There was some solid progress at the same time in the fields of education, health and public works generally, though this was by no means as rapid as it might be. One commentator argued:

> Having climbed the psychological summit of a regained self-rule, Africans could at last begin to see what they could scarcely have seen earlier: the traps in which they were caught by a persistence of late-colonial institutions and relationships.[23]

However, for the larger problems involving international cooperation on a world scale the Commonwealth still has much to offer the African continent.

6 Conclusion

After 1947, with considerable *sang-froid,* the governors set about liquidating their powers – imprisoning the revolutionaries one moment, making them prime minister the next, and then retiring to the English countryside.
Anthony Sampson [1]

In a sense independence has come to every colonial territory both too soon and too late. Too soon for the development of the resources in personnel that are needed to solve the problems of a twentieth-century state, too late for the end of paternal rule to be attained without creating resentment and suspicion among its subjects.
L. P. Mair[2]

On 1 January, 1973, Great Britain formally entered the European Economic Community and ended its long period of what Disraeli used delicately to call its 'abstention' from Europe. The English Channel was now to be seen as a 'gateway and not a moat.' Britain thus formally recognised that if Empire was now a thing of the past the European connection was the main source of inspiration for the future. During the 1960s (the period of Britain's first and second applications to join) the six nations of Europe experienced an increase of 44 per cent in gross national product, with private consumption increased by one-third; trade between the 'Six' rose 150 per cent and real incomes increased by 25 per cent. At the same time the following table shows the increasing strength of Europe in world trade.

Europe in world trade 1972 (figures in US$ million)

	Exports	*Imports*
EEC (Six)	88,499	88,422
EEC (Nine)	114,631	119,795
USA	43,226	39,963
USSR	12,800	11,739
Japan	19,318	18,881

It was agreed that tariff barriers should be 100 per cent dismantled in five stages, by 20 per cent in April 1973, January 1974, 1975, 1976 and July 1977.

The relative decline of Commonwealth trade

Britain imports 1958 £million		*%*	*1968 £million*		*%*	*1958-68 % increase*
EEC	538	14	EEC	1551	20	188
Commonwealth	1336	35	Commonwealth	1867	24	40
Britain exports 1958 £million		*%*	*1968 £million*		*%*	*1958-68 % increase*
EEC	448	14	EEC	1196	19	167
Commonwealth	1239	38	Commonwealth	1408	23	14

Notes

1 1966-70. Trade between Commonwealth countries as a proportion of the total Commonwealth trade declined from 27 to 22 per cent.

2 Britain took 27 per cent of Australia's exports in 1960, 12 per cent in 1970.

3 Canada sent 17 per cent of her exports to Britain in 1960, 9 per cent in 1970.

By 1974, only 15 per cent of Britain's exports went to the Commonwealth.

No doubt, even before 1973, the Commonwealth often looked from the vantage point of European London to be poor, difficult and sometimes ungrateful. Even Australia, which was Britain's best Commonwealth customer, has a population only slightly larger than that of Paris and Rome combined. Had Britain not entered the EEC two unenviable economic situations would have faced her. First, she would have progressively experienced the full force of European tariffs (without necessarily receiving aid from the Americans); secondly, she would have had to try to maintain a gradually declining system of preferences. At the same time, moreover, many Commonwealth countries were already increasing their trade with Europe, and came to seek associate membership with the EEC while still remaining within the Commonwealth. For example, under the Arusha agreement of 1969 (which came into force on 1 January, 1971), three East African countries, Kenya, Uganda and Tanzania, became associated with the EEC; Nigeria on the west coast entered into association in 1966; the former French West African states have been associated since 1963. However, the Commonwealth is not merely an economic proposition and clearly it could never recover effectively from the trauma of British withdrawal should this become the reality of Community membership.

As late as 1965, it was possible for middle-aged men to stand up at political meetings and get a cheer by declaring themselves to be unrepentant believers in the Empire. After the mid-1970s the term 'British Empire' will be found only in history books. Whereas in 1945 over 600 million people in the Empire were ruled from the Colonial and India Offices in London, by 1965 there was no more than a residual obligation to rule 15 million, a third of whom were in Hong Kong.

For Britain the end of Empire has presented many difficult and serious political problems which do not appear even now to be easily solved. In the first place, Britain is unlikely to make a firm decision to wind up the Commonwealth, nor is any particularly strong emotional attachment to Europe probable. The policy is likely to be one of drifting into an uneasy situation in which Britain has reservations about her role both in Europe and in the Commonwealth. Britain's economic future may lie in Europe but it will only slowly divest itself of its past. Britain is still regarded by many in the older Dominions (including English-speaking South Africans) as a cultural homeland, and former colonies which have inherited British institutions and practices still 'think British'.

Secondly, residual problems of Empire are still likely to compel Britain to be involved in problems which she would prefer not to have to handle, In a sense, the whole question of 'coloured' immigration to Britain is a visible and everyday issue in Britain itself. The Rhodesian situation is bound to remain contentious because it is now part of an intractable international situation, relating to a country where Britain has responsibility without the power to intervene. The reversion of Hong Kong's New Territories to China in 1997 will require much patient negotiation with a China which has itself a number of difficult questions to solve in the post-Mao era.

Thirdly, the Commonwealth will remain a fact of international political life. Meetings will be held which will rehearse the larger international issues in which Britain will be involved. At the same time Britain will be the initiator of cooperative ventures involving the many specialised agencies of Commonwealth cooperation which have been built up over the years from education to ecology and from fishing to law reform. The Commonwealth will move from the 'politics' of men to the 'administration' of things.

In order to appreciate something of the immense changes which the former British Empire has experienced in the past twenty-five years, it will be of some value to compare some elements in the legal situation then and now. In 1931 the Statute of Westminster gave legal formulation to the independence of the Dominions and is quite properly regarded as an important development in imperial history. By the early 1970s the Commonwealth had become a loose and unsystematic grouping of highly disparate states.

The following table provides a summary illustration of the contrasting position of the Commonwealth in 1931 and 1975.

	Empire 1931	*Commonwealth 1975*
1	Full responsible government to five Dominions, subject to external prerogatives of the King (e.g. declaration of war).	No control on any of the policies of the thirty-three independent members. Australia fought a war in Vietnam. India and Pakistan fight four wars after independence. Uganda confronts Tanzania.
2	Governor-General is the King's representative with a secure constitutional position.	Commonwealth has majority of republican presidents. Queen is formally 'Head of the Commonwealth'.
3	Imperial (British) Parliament pre-eminent over all the other parliaments in the Empire (Statute of Westminster)	Full independence of each Commonwealth parliament (or president or frequently, military ruler). Entrenched clauses repealed

contd.

Empire 1931	Commonwealth 1975
(Example: Entrenched clauses in South African Constitution preserving franchise rights of Cape Coloureds).	1952 by South African Parliament (with a Nationalist party majority).
4 The Privy Council is the highest law court of appeal in the Empire.	Only the few remaining colonies and New Zealand still retain the Privy Council.
5 Legislative powers to prevent interimperial conflict.	Commonwealth countries follow independent lines of policy as determined by national considerations. Interstate disputes in Central Africa, East Africa, Nigeria (Biafra), Cyprus.
6 Lawyers argue that members of Empire require King's agreement before leaving the Empire/Commonwealth.	Eire leaves 1949. ('In the name of the Most Holy Trinity'). Burma leaves 1947. South Africa leaves 1961. Rhodesia, with UDI leaves 1965 (loosely in Commonwealth). Pakistan leaves 1972.

In mid-1975 the Commonwealth contained thirty-three very varied members, but this diversity was no barrier to continued membership. Those states which had chosen to leave were relatively few: Burma (1947), Eire or Southern Ireland (1949), South Africa (1961), and Pakistan (1972), Rhodesia remained in an indeterminate position, a rebel colony *within* the Commonwealth. No *colony* has ever tried to leave the Commonwealth, most had wanted to become independent states within the Commonwealth. No country had ever been expelled from the Commonwealth, though South Africa had been close to this position in the late 1950s and, at the time of Rhodesian independence in the mid-1960s, Tanzania had called for Britain's expulsion, cut off diplomatic ties with Britain but stayed in the Commonwealth. There were voices heard in British political circles which called for Uganda's expulsion in 1972-73 on the grounds of mistreatment of Uganda's Asians.

In fact, the departures have been remarkably few because most member states believe that it is not in their best interests to leave the Commonwealth. However, any state which feels its basic position threatened (as did South Africa in 1961 or Pakistan in 1972) will obviously not wish to remain a member of the Commonwealth. Speaking about Britain's position, the 'Economist' of 21 April 1973 put the matter rather more succinctly:

> Since 1971, the unwritten rule that every Commonwealth country is entirely free to pursue its own foreign policy has been made to apply to Britain as well as to the other members of the club: it is now much less likely than it was before 1971 that Britain will be dissuaded from following a course of action that suits its interests by the threat that somebody will leave the Commonwealth if it does.

On the other hand, a far more deeply rooted problem is that of a loss of feeling of close union between the members, which might be seen as a psychological malaise. There are two reasons which might help to account for this situation. First, the problems of the Commonwealth are difficult to distinguish from international problems in general. Thus the 'confrontation' between Malaysia (a Commonwealth country) and Indonesia (a non-Commonwealth country) is part of the general picture of international confrontations and in no way necessarily different in terms of international conflict from the confrontation between India and Pakistan, both, at the relevant times members of the Commonwealth. The problems of Rhodesia, Cyprus, Malta and Hong Kong, are as much part of the international scene as they are specifically Commonwealth problems.

Secondly, although Britain is the founder member of the Commonwealth she lacks the power to enforce her will on other members. While it is no doubt a progressive outlook that all should be 'free and equal members' of a unique human enterprise', the practical difficulties of this pluralistic outlook are considerable. There is no central *sovereign* power to effect central decisions in a positive and tidy fashion.

Thirdly, Britain has found herself progressively moving away from her closest kith and kin, and at the same time Australians and New Zealanders, who for long had been loyal supporters of the policies of the mother country, began after 1972 to speak of British 'colonialism', this suggested that the tradition of a benign mother country was now seen by many to be transformed into a burden rather than accepted without question as a noble heritage. In particular, Britain's stricter rules on immigration increased the difficulty of access of old Commonwealth citizens into Britain, even though in 1973 the rules for entry for citizens from Old Commonwealth countries were less stringent than those from the New.

For at least forty years the Commonwealth has been sustained on the economic base of economic preferences developed in the 1930s at Ottawa. This meant that trading between Britain and its Commonwealth was carried on at preferential rates, to the disadvantage of outsiders. British membership of the EEC was incompatible with the protection implicit in the scheme of Commonwealth preferences. In joining the EEC however, Britain took up the new option – a European tariff. Even after the establishment of the enlarged Community of Nine in 1973, Commonwealth economic problems were not fully solved. The question of Commonwealth sugar, for example, still contains a number of problems. In 1973 Britain still imported nearly 2 million tons of sugar under quotas from Commonwealth countries. At the same time the EEC had an annual sugar beet surplus of 1 million tons. Certain countries like Mauritius, Barbados and Fiji produce sugar almost to the exclusion of anything else. Under the Commonwealth Sugar Agreement, due for expiry in 1974, Britain guaranteed to buy Commonwealth sugar at a favourable price. The old Empire was to some extent built on sugar production in the eighteenth century. In the 1970s the sugar situation well illustrated the change in the imperial connection.

Commonwealth sugar supply 1973 ('000 tons)

Country	
Guyana (West Indies)	522
Australia	453
Mauritius	415
Fiji	141
Swaziland	87
India	25
British Honduras	25

Early in 1975 however, an arrangement was made to allow for Commonwealth sugar to enter Europe, and thus the British market, on special terms.

The states of the Commonwealth provide many illustrations of the ways in which political life follows subcultures and human groupings. The following ethnic confrontations are examples.

* In *Cyprus* and *Sri Lanka* we discover a majority group facing a large minority. In Cyprus, Greeks and Turks operate in the same relation to each other as do Sinhalese and Tamils.
* In *Uganda* and *Ghana,* each has a powerful central group, race or tribe (the Baganda and Ashanti), with several medium-sized groups on the periphery.
* In *Pakistan* before the creation of Bangladesh there were two evenly balanced major groups. In *Northern Ireland,* within the United Kingdom itself, there are similar problems, given the slight but significant numerical majority of Protestants over Catholics.
* In *India* the graduation of a vast variety of groups and castes within castes stretches over many social types.
* In *Tanzania* the situation is again different and may be described as one of the multiple small tribal groups, a situation in contrast with that of neighbouring Kenya with its rather more dominant controlling tribe, the Kikuyu.
* In *Rhodesia* the situation is somewhat different as a small minority group of different race (the Rhodesian whites) dominates two African groups (Shona and Ndebebe) numerically far greater than itself.
* In South Africa, a former Commonwealth member, the situation is significantly different again: there are two white groups and a number of African tribal groups as well as a significant Indian group and a group of mixed race.

The Commonwealth contains several states under the control of military men. The largest African Commonwealth country, Nigeria, for example, had a hope that civilian rule would be restored by 1976, provided future political parties can govern effectively. The Nigerian military government has been accepted with considerable sympathy in the Commonwealth. Its existence is justified on the grounds that the role of the military is to correct the abuses of politicians. A military regime is held to be accountable only to the popular revolution, without need for parliaments or other political institutions. Such an assertion is a far cry from the pre-independence claim of Nkrumah, who wrote that 'in our struggle for freedom, parliamentary democracy was as vital an aim as independence'.[3]

The whole question of military rule is very complicated. Soldiers assume political power by means of a *coup d'état.* It is true very often that soldiers remove politicians who have become corrupt, but it is sometimes forgotten that soldiers also can be corrupt. When military rule fails to provide the material advance which a poor state demands it too will be threatened. In some cases the military group has returned power to civilian politicians (as in Ghana and Sierra Leone); there can also be second *coups* which remove the restored civilian politicians in favour of new soldiery, as in Ghana.

There is no simple reason why *coups* occur. There are *coups* of the Left and *coups* of the Right; there are *coups* in favour of a particular religion or a particular ideology; there are *coups* which are essentially tribal and those which are essentially economic. We can mention *coups* in Ghana (1966 and 1972), in Lesotho (1970), in Nigeria (January 1966 and July 1966), in Sierra Leone (1967 and 1968), in Uganda (1966 and 1971), as well as in Pakistan (1958). Only when the army is fully loyal to the civilian government can it be accepted that there is no imminent possibility of a *coup.* Many of the states of the New Commonwealth are poor, often dependent on a single crop for their economic resources, subject to a high degree of illiteracy and possibly sickness. There may be conflicts between those who support traditional values and those who may be described as modernisers. Political institutions may be largely unsuccessful or undeveloped in these states. They are therefore prone to *coups.* A *coup,* of course, will not always be successful, but when it is the whole administrative apparatus of the state is absorbed into the army. Many of the military rulers of the Commonwealth were trained at the Royal Military Academy, Sandhurst, and many jokes have been made regarding the importance of Sandhurst as a nursery of Commonwealth politicians. Britain trained her colonies to follow the Westminster model of parliament, cabinet and incorrupt civil service. No one dreamt before 1960 that the fate of so many states would be in the hands of military men.

One military coup, that which overthrew Nkrumah in Ghana, has been dealt with by Colonel A.A. Afrifa in his book, *The Ghana Coup.* Of his Sandhurst training, Colonel Afrifa wrote:

> Now I look back on Sandhurst with nostalgia. . . . It is an institution that teaches that all men are equal, that the profession of men-at-arms is essential, and a peaceful one. It shows the stupidity of racial

> conflicts, and the joy of the communion of all men in the service of peace.'. . . Sandhurst gave us independent thinking, tolerance and a liberal outlook. . . . There was no discrimination whatsoever.[4]

Allowing for possible exaggerations there is still in these statements, a clear appreciation of British military rather than ordinary administrative training. We must expect a considerable number of Commonwealth states to continue to be ruled by soldiers.

One of the curious features of the Commonwealth, particularly as regards Africa, is that it accepts the single-party state as well as parliamentary forms which suggest Government and Opposition. Nyerere argued that a multiparty system was a luxury which Africa could not afford on account of antinational and tribal tendencies, though he also warned that high quality leadership was essential for the one-party system to succeed. Yet there was a continuing interest shown in parliaments. In 1911 parliamentary representatives from Britain and the five dominions met in London at the time of the coronation of King George V; by 1961 there were sixty-one representatives of Commonwealth parliaments and by 1973 there were ninety-four. At the Commonwealth Parliamentary Conference held in September 1973 there were 121 delegates, including ninety-four national state and provincial Commonwealth legislatures. It would be wrong no doubt, to see parliaments as equals in terms of power with parties in modern Africa, but it would equally be wrong to eliminate parliaments from the political reckoning altogether.

An interesting question has been posed regarding the measurement of 'democracy' in a number of states. One investigation, when applied to the Commonwealth, has produced the following result.

Fifteen Commonwealth states ranked according to degree of political democracy (1946-1965)

State	*Score*
Australia	137.7
New Zealand	137.7
United Kingdom	131.6
India	107.1
Trinidad-Tobago	105-0
Malaysia	103.8
Sierra Leone	102.9

contd.

State	*Score*
Uganda*	102.0
Nigeria	100.0
Cyprus	96.4
Tanzania	94.0
Ghana	91.0
Kenya	86.5
Malawi	83.2
Pakistan (now left)	72.8

* Before Uganda's deportation of Asians

(Adapted from A. K. Smith, Jr, 'Socio-economic development and political democracy: a causal analysis', *Midwest Journal of Political Science,* February 1969, pp. 104-5).

It is clear that some Commonwealth states are more democratic than others; they have therefore absorbed their British heritage in different ways. The Old Commonwealth states show this heritage more obviously than the new, and each one tries to demonstrate its uniqueness by an inclination to assert its nationalism. All the Commonwealth states utilise their newly found sense of national consciousness as a tool of political power in the world of international politics.

What the Commonwealth hopes to achieve is to harness national self-interest for the greater benefit of its members and their inhabitants. Nevertheless emergent nationalism is the biggest single threat to its continuance. Provided the Commonwealth can contain these nationalisms it has still a useful role to play in world affairs.

Appendices

Appendix A

Members of The Commonwealth of Nations 1975 (assumed to have commenced with Statute of Westminster, 1931)

1 Independent members

State	*Date of independence*	*Population*	*Area (sq. miles)*	*Average GNP US$*	*Government and politics*
United Kingdom	31 Dec 1931	55,068,000	94,214	2200	Parliamentary, two party
Australia	31 Dec 1931	11,751,000	2,971,081	2550	Parliamentary, two party
New Zealand	31 Dec 1931	2,726,000	103,736	2815	Parliamentary, two party
Canada	31 Dec 1931	20,411,000	3,851,809	3350	Parliamentary, two party
(R) India	15 Aug 1947	511,115,000	1,176,252	80	Parliamentary, Congress Party dominates
(R) (West) Pakistan	15 Aug 1947	107,258,000	310,403	125	Presidential, left Commonwealth 1971
(R) Sri Lanka	4 Feb 1948	11,491,000	25,332	160	Parliamentary, multiparty
(R) Ghana	3 June 1957	8,143,000	92,100	250	Military rule
(R) Nigeria	1 Oct 1960	58,600,000	365,699	75	Military rule
(R) Cyprus	13 March 1961	616,000	3,572	800	Turk/Cypriot, multiparty
(R) Sierra Leone	27 April 1961	2,439,000	27,925	150	Confused parliamentary, some military interference
Jamaica	6 Aug 1962	1,876,000	4,411	620	Parliamentary, two party
Trinidad } Tobago }	31 Aug 1962 31 Aug 1962	1,000,000	1,980	730	Single party has all 36 seats

(R) Uganda	9 Oct 1962	7,740,000	91,134	110	Military rule
Malaysia	16 Sept 1963	9,855,000	128,328	350	Federal, multiparty
(R) Kenya	12 Dec 1963	9,948,000	224,960	130	*De facto* single party
(R) Tanzania	26 April 1964	12,231,342	362,844	70	Single party
(R) Malawi	6 July 1964	4,042,412	45,747	60	Single party
(R) Malta	21 Sept 1964	318,000	122	670	Parliamentary two party
(R) Zambia	24 Oct 1964	3,894,000	290,724	400	Single-party
Gambia	18 Feb 1965	343,000	4,003	100	*De facto* single party
(R) Singapore	16 Oct 1965	1,956,000	225	840	*De facto* single party
(R) Guyana	26 May 1966	662,000	83,000	330	Parliamentary, multiparty
(R) Botswana	30 Sept 1966	593,000	222,000	95	Dominant party
Lesotho	4 Oct 1966	852,459	11,716	85	Dominant party, own monarchy
Barbados	30 Nov 1966	254,000	166	480	Parliamentary, multiparty
Mauritius	12 March 1968	795,000	787	220	Parliamentary, multiparty
Swaziland	6 Sept 1968	374,700	2,000	165	Dominant party, own monarchy
Tonga	4 June 1970	79,000	270	none available	Undeveloped party, own monarchy
Fiji	10 Oct 1970	490,000	7,055	370	Coalition on strict proportional representation
(R) Bangladesh (est)	4 Feb 1971	72,000,000	55,126	75	Dominant party, Awami League
Bahamas	9 July 1973	169,000	5,382		Parliamentary multiparty

(R) denotes Republic

2 Dependencies

State	*Population*	*Area* (sq. miles)
Antigua	61,000	170
Bermuda	52,000	21
British Antarctic	nil	666,000
British Honduras (Belize)	120,000	8,867
Indian Ocean Territories	2,000	30
British Solomon Islands	147,000	11,500
Virgin Islands	10,500	59
Brunei	107,000	2,226
Canton and Enderbery Islands	320	27
Cayman Islands	9,000	100
Central and Southern Line Islands	nil	43
Dominica	70,000	290
Falkland Islands	2,000	4,618
Gibraltar	27,000	2
Gilbert and Ellice Islands	57,000	369
Grenada	99,000	120
Hong Kong	3,990,000	399
Montserrat	15,000	38
New Hebrides	78,000	5,700
Pitcairn Islands	92	2
St Christopher-Nevis-Anguilla	60,000	136
St Helena	5,000	47
St Lucia	105,000	238
St Vincent	91,000	150
Seychelles	51,000	55
Turks and Caicos Islands	6,000	166

(Rhodesia is regarded as a British dependency but does not effectively function as a Commonwealth member. Population 5,100,000; area 150,820 sq. miles.)

State	*Population*	*Area* (sq. miles)
Dependencies (Australian)		
Ashmore and Cartier Islands	nil	77
Australian Antarctic territories	nil	2,362,875
Christmas Island	3,000	55
Cocos Islands	1,000	5
Heard and McDonald Islands	nil	200
Norfolk Islands	1,000	13
Papua and New Guinea	2,220,000	183,540
Dependencies (New Zealand)		
Cook Islands	20,000	90
Niue	5,000	100
Ross Dependency	nil	160,000
Tokelau Islands	2,000	4
Dependencies (India)		
Sikkim	187,000	2,818

Appendix B

Map of the Commonwealth

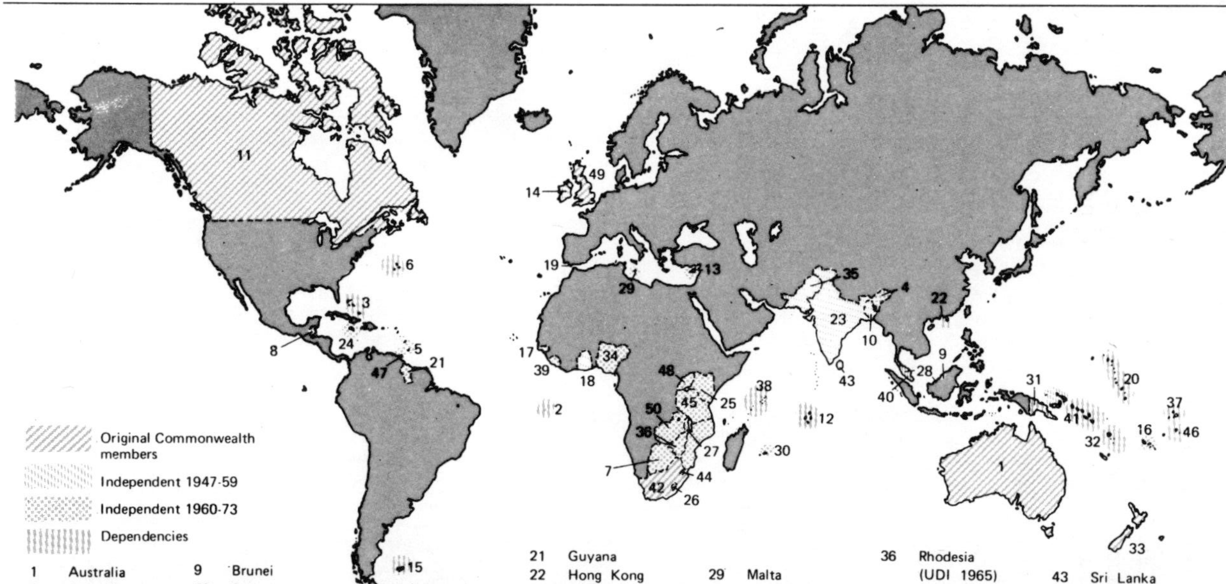

- Original Commonwealth members
- Independent 1947-59
- Independent 1960-73
- Dependencies

1 Australia
2 Ascension
3 Bahamas
4 Bangladesh
5 Barbados
6 Bermuda
7 Botswana
8 British Honduras
9 Brunei
10 Burma (left 1947)
11 Canada
12 Chagos
13 Cyprus
14 Eire (left 1949)
15 Falklands
16 Fiji
17 Gambia
18 Ghana
19 Gibraltar
20 Gilbert and Ellice Islands
21 Guyana
22 Hong Kong
23 India
24 Jamaica
25 Kenya
26 Lesotho
27 Malawi
28 Malaysia (Federation of 1963)
29 Malta
30 Mauritius
31 New Guinea
32 New Hebrides
33 New Zealand
34 Nigeria
35 Pakistan (left 1972)
36 Rhodesia (UDI 1965)
37 Samoa
38 Seychelles
39 Sierra Leone
40 Singapore
41 Solomons
42 South Africa (left 1961)
43 Sri Lanka
44 Swaziland
45 Tanzania
46 Tonga
47 Trinidad
48 Uganda
49 United Kingdom
50 Zambia

Appendix C

This Commonwealth Declaration was approved unanimously, after thorough discussion and careful consideration, at the Heads of Government Meeting in Singapore in January 1971.

The issuing of the Declaration was seen as something of an historic development because it was the first time that the Commonwealth countries had spelt out in detail the principles they share.

Declaration of Commonwealth Principles

Agreed by Commonwealth Heads of Government meeting at Singapore, 22 January 1971, and reaffirmed in April 1975.

The Commonwealth of Nations is a voluntary association of independent sovereign States, each responsible for its own policies, consulting and co-operating in the common interests of their peoples and in the promotion of international understanding and world peace.

Members of the Commonwealth come from territories in the six continents and five oceans, include peoples of different races, languages and religions, and display every stage of economic development from poor developing nations to wealthy industrialized nations. They encompass a rich variety of cultures, traditions and institutions.

Membership of the Commonwealth is compatible with the freedom of member-Governments to be non-aligned or to belong to any other grouping, association or alliance. Within this diversity all members of the Commonwealth hold certain principles in common. It is by pursuing these principles that the Commonwealth can continue to influence international society for the benefit of mankind.

We believe that international peace and order are essential to the security and prosperity of mankind; we therefore support the United Nations and seek to strengthen its influence for peace in the world, and its efforts to remove the causes of tension between nations.

We believe in the liberty of the individual, in equal rights for all citizens regardless of race, colour, creed or political belief, and in their inalienable right to participate by means of free and democratic political processes in framing the society in which they live. We therefore strive to promote in each of our countries those representative institutions and guarantees for personal freedom under the laws that are our common heritage.

We recognize racial prejudice as a dangerous sickness threatening the healthy development of the human race and racial discrimination as an unmitigated evil of society. Each of us will vigorously combat this evil within our own nation.

No country will afford to regimes which practise racial discrimination assistance which in its own judgment directly contributes to the pursuit or consolidation of this evil policy. We oppose all forms of colonial domination and racial oppression and are committed to the principles of human dignity and equality.

We will therefore use all our efforts to foster human equality and dignity everywhere, and to further the principles of self-determination and non-racialism.

We believe that the wide disparities in wealth now existing between different sections of mankind are too great to be tolerated. They also create world tensions. Our aim is their progressive removal. We therefore seek to use our efforts to overcome poverty, ignorance and disease, in raising standards of life and achieving a more equitable international society.

To this end our aim is to achieve the freest possible flow of international trade on terms fair and equitable to all, taking into account the special requirements of the developing countries, and to encourage the flow of adequate resources, including governmental and private resources, to the developing countries, bearing in mind the importance of doing this in a true spirit of partnership and of establishing for this purpose in the developing countries conditions which are conducive to sustain investment and growth.

We believe that international co-operation is essential to remove the causes of war, promote tolerance, combat injustice, and secure development among the peoples of the world. We are convinced that the Commonwealth is one of the most fruitful associations for these purposes.

In pursuing these principles the members of the Commonwealth believe that they can provide a constructive example of the multinational approach which is vital to peace and progress in the modern world. The association is based on consultation, discussion and co-operation.

In rejecting coercion as an instrument of policy they recognise that the security of each member-State from external aggression is a matter of concern to all members. It provides many channels for continuing exchanges of knowledge and views on professional, cultural, economic, legal and political issues among member-States.

These relationships we intend to foster and extend, for we believe that our multi-national association can expand human understanding and understanding among nations, assist in the elimination of discrimination based on differences of race, colour or creed, maintain and strengthen personal liberty, contribute to the enrichment of life for all, and provide a powerful influence for peace among nations.

Appendix D

Newspaper reports of the Commonwealth Prime Ministers' Conference in Ottawa (August 1973)

1 The sceptical

'Well, who wants this black and white show?'
John Dickinson, *London Evening News*, 7 August, 1973

At the height of this Heads of Government conference, the question has suddenly ceased to be: does Britain lead the Commonwealth any more?

It has become much more: who, in Heaven's name, will take over this very unwelcome role?

Obviously, Canada's Mr. Trudeau is prepared to be the figurehead for the time being.

He has virtually no Parliamentary majority and stage management on the world scene gives him some dubious second-hand glory at home.

Mr. Heath, who should be the traditional inheritor of leadership looks about as enthusiastic as a man bequeathed a broken-down property with an expensive mortgage.

As one senior French observer said today: 'He seems so obviously to despise it all'.

When the Commonwealth leaders first assembled here, most people were asking solemnly whether the Commonwealth in its present form could survive.

This is no longer the serious question.

As an organisation, it is all too plainly quite indestructible

Whatever happens over Britain transferring her activities into Europe, the Commonwealth will trudge on as one of the most durable, and probably one of the most boring, associations in world politics.

But at almost every meeting point in debate there are collisions and frictions.

All the Commonwealth nations go on squabbling amiably among themselves and the Afro-Asian powers are now fighting between themselves, perhaps more energetically than any others.

Mr. Heath has already taken a great bash at Uganda over the expulsion of the Asians.

Not content with this, he is committed to a repeat performance before the conference ends on Friday.

Mr. Trudeau has just given a party for delegates, where the music was supplied by a band from the Royal Canadian Mounted Police and the lighting was from chandeliers taken from Liverpool Town Hall.

But Mr. Heath has also called the great 'kith and kin' leader, Australia's Mr. Gough Whitlam a perpetrator of 'economic nationalism'.

And the Australians and New Zealanders are getting ready to head the Afro-Asian attack on Britain over Rhodesia.

Mr. Heath has also accused the Indian leaders here of economic ignorance and of failing 'to understand the position accurately' on Britain's financial policies.

The occasion was marked by some spectacular private punch-ups.

Not the least of these was between Nigeria's leader, Gen. Gowon, and the new boy from Bangladesh, Sheik Mujibur Rahman.

General Gowon, still smarting over the Biafran civil war, made it plain he had no time for breakaway minority movements.

The dialogue was crisp and to the point. It went like this:

The Sheik: 'You are a General and I am a politician.'

Gowon: 'I am both a General and a politician!'

The Sheik (holding up his hands to Gowon's): 'Look at our skin –they are almost the same colour!'

It was an episode which illustrated vividly much of the atmosphere here.

2 The optimistic

'Talking heads – a Commonwealth success.'
Patrick Keatley, *The Guardian,* 11 August, 1973

The 1973 Commonwealth summit conference has been a level-headed success. That is the verdict not only of the 32 delegations, but also of the majority of correspondents covering this enormous gathering.

My own description of it would be the 'Cool Conference.' For here in this northern capital, the Canadians have organised something that is distinctively different from all that has gone before. The Nigerian leader, Jack Gowon, the 38-year-old army general turned politician, seemed to hit exactly the right description for it when he spoke about 'The Spirit of Ottawa.'

How would you define it? I have put this point to many of the delegations, including the Prime Ministers and Presidents who lead them. What emerges is this.

The Commonwealth conference here has been even-tempered, in spite of the hard arguments on nuclear tests at the beginning and the perhaps inevitable battle about what to do over Rhodesia at the end. It has been informal, in the Canadian manner and thus utterly different from the traditional rigidities when these meetings are held in London at Marlborough House. It has been a week and a half of personal encounters, quite apart from high politics, where people have fairly bubbled with goodwill, the kind of thing that old-timers hazily recall from the days of the Commonwealth summits in the far off 1950s, before the advent of the apartheid battles at the conferences of 1960-1 when South Africa was forced to withdraw.

The ordinary voter is entitled to ask what his country has got out of it. I suppose the short answer is to say that these summits help to make the world a safer place, a more tolerant place when it comes to the tensions between the races, and perhaps a more prosperous place because of the discussions on trade, aid and development.

But if you want a more precise category of immediate achievements in terms of projects, there were plenty of them as well. This came about when the 32 governments turned to what they call their 'housekeeping budget'.

Because it is not often realised that these Commonwealth conferences are really two things wrapped together in one package lasting nine or ten days. On the one hand, it is a gathering of leaders of totally sovereign nations who owe each other nothing in terms of foreign policy. For the Commonwealth is not a treaty organisation; it is not a military, trading or diplomatic bloc. Its members pursue highly individual goals in foreign policy, ranging from those like Tanzania who have close links with China to the white nations, Britain and Canada, in NATO and other parts of the global power game of the Western bloc. But, as one former New Zealand Prime Minister once put it, membership of the Commonwealth is 'independence plus'. But, paradoxically, this is precisely its value to the tough-minded men and women who come here. They pose for the traditional picture with the Queen, as they did here in Ottawa at Government House. And this somehow conveys the false impression that these summits are some kind of glorified tea party. Yet one has only to think of Mr Heath's role in British life or Mr Trudeau here in Canada, to realise that these people are as tough as they come in the tough business of politics. They run a Cabinet, they head a government, and most important of all they are party bosses. And they seem to find that being able to go into a small friendly room, behind closed doors, with few others present, and having a real interchange of arguments and data on the big issues facing the world, is something of immeasurable value to them.

And this time, at the 1973 conference, mercifully they have been able to do all this in an atmosphere of genuine goodwill. This was possible because the highly emotional issue of Southern Africa had reached a kind of plateau – perhaps temporary – where the leaders seem to agree that Britain had done practically everything she could do for the moment and the political ball is in the court of Ian Smith and Bishop Muzorewa of the ANC. Of course, there were some new and ingenious ideas as one would expect on the possible initiatives which could be taken on a negotiated settlement, notably those put forward by the Prime Minister of Barbados, Mr Erroll Barrow. But there was no crisis topic like that of Singapore in 1971, when there was a move of desperation to pull Britain back from the brink over arms sales to South Africa.

On the housekeeping side, thanks to this cool and constructive atmosphere, we have seen handsome increases in appropriations for the many projects which are shared by Commonwealth countries in such fields as education, technical assistance, and economic development. Britain and Canada gave the lead with increased commitments to the

Commonwealth Foundation, the Technical Fund, and fresh commitments to the new Commonwealth Youth plan. There were many more, down a long list. But perhaps the intangible is the best way of all to convey the new mood achieved by this conference. When some of us were leaving the party at the very end, we found ourselves falling into step with the particular Prime Minister who had stayed longer than all the others, having talked with almost all of them, and was now leaving last of all. It was the new, relaxed, highly inter-racial Ted Heath, who had been enjoying himself thoroughly. It was all light years away from the angry clashes of Singapore two years ago.

3 The pragmatic

'All smiles as Heath leaves for Cowes'
Robert Carvel, *London Evening Standard,* 9 August, 1973

What a change. Mr Heath leaves for home tonight with nearly everyone wishing him luck for the Fastnet race and with him saying how splendid the Commonwealth organisation is after all.

The British delegation is rightly relieved. With good reason, Whitehall had feared a great punch-up between Ted at his most abrasive and some wild-eyed African leaders in their most prickly anti-imperialist mood.

But what did we get? Tanzania's President Julius Nyerere all smiles for our Prime Minister and actually referring to the foreign secretary as 'my brother Alec'. The ex-14th earl who has so many relatives already delightedly acknowledged this new one.

Before leaving for Ottawa the Prime Minister had scarcely concealed his impatience, even contempt, for this Commonwealth gathering.

Having endured sustained Brit-bashing and general abuse at the 1971 Singapore conference he arrived here an apprehensive man very much on edge.

Of course things have turned out much better than he expected.

For a start the huge, unspeakable Idi Amin was too scared to leave Uganda to attend. Also tiny, tiresome Hastings Banda of Malawi stayed at home. Other fireworks merchants like Zambia's Kenneth Kaunda were absent. So Britain's tormentors were not at full strength.

But what mattered more was that the Africans in particular are now adopting a more sophisticated low-key diplomacy.

This gave much more of a chance for reasonable discussion. However, what I believe is really sending Mr Heath home a lot happier is something very human. He has taken a chance to shine.

The new conference format aimed at avoiding set speeches and providing for more informal exchanges worked to the British leader's advantage simply because he grew up as a political operator at Westminster where it pays to be a master of the impromptu.

As a result he did more talking than most. 'Britain treated the Commonwealth with benign neglect', teased Singapore's Lee Kwan Yew. 'Benign yes, neglect never', flashed Mr. Heath. Other delegations without one hundred per cent Oxbridge background thought he was ever so clever.

Now Mr Heath travels home talking about ideas for making the next Commonwealth Conference an even more useful event and he just will not have it that, as Mr Lee suggests, Britain joining the Common Market has torn the guts out of the Commonwealth. Of course, Mr Heath's first love is still the EEC – make no mistakes.

But apart from the more civilised tone of the Ottawa meeting of the 32 heads of government, the Prime Minister probably now realises more clearly that the old Empire lands – many now so aggressively independent – hold the key to continued western prosperity because they produce so many of the world's essentials in food and minerals and are realising they have strength to exploit.

So, thinks Mr Heath, he had better sound a bit more friendly. And as it turned out nobody was very unfriendly to him. Nyerere was even relaxed enough last night to mimic ex-Colonial Secretary Duncan Sandys.

The new men from down under – Australia's Gough Whitlam and Norman Kirk of New Zealand – have pleased Mr Heath not a bit. In the British delegation the former is suspected of acting as a kind of barrack room lawyer for some of the smaller countries. The Australian leader is of course a real lawyer.

With host Premier Trudeau and Mrs Bandaranaike of Sri Lanka (Ceylon, that was) Mr Heath has got on particularly well.

Mrs Bandaranaike went so far as to thank Britain for some things and wish us well in the Common Market. When she comes to London next, Mr Heath will be giving her a rose – as he did in the front hall at Number Ten when India's Mrs Gandhi last called.

I am told she was terribly pleased – not expecting such a thing from a middle-aged batchelor.

As well as Mr Heath, Mr Trudeau will be annoyed with Mr. Whitlam.

The Australian has pre-recorded a television interview to be shown in Canada and by the BBC tonight, and in it he forecasts both Canada and Australia will eventually become republics.

Mr Trudeau has spent a lot of time lately trying to show what a good monarchist he is and by having the Queen here he has hoped to strengthen a political position weakened by the fears of many English speaking Canadians that Frenchy Trudeau is not their friend.

Today Mr Heath had to make his speech on Rhodesia before flying home overnight – in good time for his Cowes race.

The Rhodesia debate began in a restrained way with Nyerere demanding no settlement without African majority rule. However, the Tanzanian leader agreed that General Amin must be condemned for racialism as much as any white settlers.

I do not expect Mr Heath to have much trouble in setting out Britain's case.

He has already discovered Nigeria's General Gowon pretty helpful. 'That military gentleman was in London recently, wasn't he?' one cynical delegate said. 'He's had the Royal treatment of course. You can see the results.'

Whatever all the reasons for the better conference atmosphere – and the Queen played her part here at the beginning – it is probably right to say that the unique forum for consultation between white, black, brown and yellow races and rich and poor nations which the Commonwealth provides has again justified its existence.

Appendix E

Commonwealth Maturity: two Canadian views

1 Extract from an address by the Secretary of State for External Affairs, the Hon. Mitchell Sharp, to the Commonwealth Association of Architects, Ottawa, 5 November 1973, referring to the Commonwealth Heads of Government Conference 1973

Over the past twenty years, to use extravagant language such as excellent, or extraordinarily successful, to describe a Commonwealth heads of government conference would have invited accusations of being, at best, diplomatic to a fault or, at worst, dishonest. However, this conference *was* excellent. And this was not because it was held in Canada or because the Canadian Prime Minister or the Canadian delegation dominated the proceedings. It was partly because no one person or issue dominated the proceedings. As Prime Minister Trudeau said at the time: 'I think there is what I would almost describe as a beautiful equality. The people who get the most done are those who make the brightest interventions and on one subject it might be one country and on another it might be another.' All leaders had their say, and it would be invidious to pick out star performers.

A most striking aspect of this past heads of government conference was the change from the meeting held in Singapore in 1971. That meeting was marked by acrimonious and protracted debate, chiefly over the question of the sale of arms to South Africa. As that debate developed, so the did risk of a Commonwealth polarised in large part along racial lines into antagonistic camps. In contrast, the Ottawa meeting was relaxed. It allowed easy and frank exchange of views. It was an atmosphere in which *rapport* and understanding between the leaders had an opportunity to develop – and this, more than specific agenda items, is one of the primary objectives of a heads of government meeting.

But how was this change brought about? The answer lies partly in careful preparation – in applying the lessons of past conferences to the framing of new ground rules. The decision to exclude all but the most immediate advisers from the heads of government discussions had a very beneficial effect. There was no gallery for anyone to play to. It enabled the heads of government to have more direct, frank and spontaneous communication with one another.

Another primary reason for the success of the conference was that finally it seems to have been accepted that the modern Commonwealth does not revolve around Britain even though that country, which was once the imperial power, will always have a special place that cannot be filled by any other country. However while this new maturity of the Commonwealth has been recognised at the top, there is still a task to be accomplished in persuading political figures, officials and editorialists in the member countries not to identify their relations with Britain. . . .

As the Ottawa conference developed, Britain became accepted more and more as an equal member. This meant that the heads of government were able to deal with real problems and not the old emotional battles that had so often prevented them from getting a constructive grip on substantive issues.

. . . I have concentrated . . . on the new maturity of the heads of government meetings. This maturity was important not just for the successful outcome of the last meeting but important for the future of our unique association.

2 Extracts from an address by Mr Marcel Cadieux, Canadian Ambassador to the United States, to the International Relations Club, Seattle, 20 September, 1973

A journalist covering the recent meeting of Commonwealth heads of government in Ottawa complained to Her Majesty the Queen that the name of this strange organisation – 'Commonwealth' – didn't really convey any idea of its nature or purposes. 'Well' Her Majesty observed dryly, 'we used to have another name for it.' It is perhaps because the Commonwealth is a lineal descendant of the British Empire that many people in the world think of it – if, indeed, they think of it at all – as a British club, with some of the anachronistic quaintness that is the charm of so many of the older clubs of London.

Historically, of course, the origins of the Commonwealth *are* in the British Empire, even if the evolution was by no means inevitable or even logical. Other colonies have developed into independent states without continuing any similar association among themselves and with their former rulers, although it is perhaps not too farfetched to see, in the recent encouragement by France of La Francophonie as an international community, a realisation of the value of such associations. Another unifying factor almost too obvious to be mentioned is, of course, a common language. The recent conference in Ottawa is surely one of the few world meetings to span so wide an area and represent so many hundreds of millions of the world's people where there was no need for interpreters. To have a common language, together with many common traditions of government, law, education, and culture, does make it possible for Commonwealth leaders to talk together with perhaps a greater degree of genuine understanding than is possible in any other world forum. . . .

For Canada, the Commonwealth is important for a number of reasons. It is, of course, a part of our history – and if our British friends claim the credit for its invention I think we can claim with equal truth that the Commonwealth evolved from the unique process of amicable decolonisation that brought Canada to a peaceful independence. It is also, in a very real sense, one of our primary windows on the world. It is an illogical organisation, with no constitution, no primary function and no defined world role. Perhaps for that very reason it can bring together statesmen from every part of the world – not to agree, not to solve world problems, not to create a new world order, but simply to exchange views and understand each other better. For Canada, and perhaps also for most of the other countries making up the Commonwealth that neither are nor aspire to be great powers, this is perhaps sufficient reason to value the nebulous Commonwealth association. . . .

Appendix F

Newspaper report of the Commonwealth Prime Ministers' Conference in Kingston (May 1975)

'Mr Wilson's nine day wonder' Michael Leapman *The Times* 7 May 1975

The last rum punch has soaked its way into the last overfed diplomatic belly. The last secret has been leaked, the last posture posed, the last i dotted in the communiqué. Commonwealth government heads are rolling back to the real world. What are the gains and losses of their nine days in Jamaica? Specifically, what are the gains and losses for our own Harold Wilson?

Wilson, as he keeps reminding us, has had more experience of these meetings than most, and knows well how to exploit them to his advantage. For him, the gains certainly outnumbered the losses.

Several images of Wilson stick in the mind – of him wielding a cigar of Churchillian length at the opening party and, at another party, mercilessly teasing an earnest American reporter trying to get a story out of him. Then sitting hunched over his radio at the weekend, listening to the Cup Final, while most other premiers disported themselves on the beach.

But my – and possibly his – most surprising memory is of the party (most memories of this conference will, I think, turn out to be of parties) given by the Governor-General on the penultimate night. The heads of government were announced over the loudspeaker as they arrived and only two were applauded by the guests. One was the ever-popular revolutionary Julius Nyerere, the other the indestructible old trouper Wilson. Nobody has been able to explain this phenomenon satisfactorily.

Wilson had most of what he wanted from the conference. His commodities plan was regarded by most as more realistic than Forbes Burnham's rival strategy to save the world. He had little trouble with militant Africans over Rhodesia and he won their approval of his plan to send a minister to parley with the white regime there.

He also made a popular contribution to the discussion towards the end on comparative techniques of government – a topic which I ridiculed, I now think rather unfairly, in my opening dispatch from here. He spoke about the political advisers the Labour Party had inserted into the Civil Service machine, and his talk so interested delegates that there was a move to return to discussion of it after the communiqué had been approved.

It also must have been a comfort for him to have Commonwealth support for Britain's continued membership of the European Community placed so unambiguously on the record, though he was careful to insist that he had not solicited this directly. (He was also lucky, as we all were, to have a valid excuse for absenting himself for nine days from the tedium of the referendum campaign.)

The Jamaicans can congratulate themselves on the smooth organization of the conference, apart from some slight trouble early on with the electricity supply and the breakdown of a crucial stapling machine at communiqué time. Security was thorough but not oppressive, and not a head of government was lost. Communications arrangements for the press worked excellently.

Nobody now claims that these conferences are either of overwhelming importance and interest, or of no importance and interest. Most of us look forward with equanimity to the next, which will be held in London in 1977. That, incidentally, was another significant gain for Wilson, for if he survives in office long enough to play host in 1977, he should be able to manipulate matters at least as successfully as he has done this time, which cannot at all harm his chances in the general election which by then will not be far away.

Appendix G

Brief comments on Empire and Commonwealth

* 'It may be fairly questioned whether the possession of India does or ever can increase our power and our security, while there is no doubt that it vastly increases our dangers and responsibilities.'
  Sir John Seeley, *The Expansion of England* (Macmillan 1883 p.13).

* 'The Dominions could not exist if it were not for the British Navy.'
  W. M. Hughes, Prime Minister of Australia, 1921.

* 'The Commonwealth continues to exist as a fluctuating association of unequal partner states, whom accidents of history have thrown together.'
  G. G. Graham, *A Concise History of the British Empire,* Thames & Hudson, 1970, p. 270.

* [It was an] 'ill-defended, ill-organised, ill-developed and immensely vulnerable empire.'
  Correlli Barnett, *The Collapse of British Power,* Eyre Methuen, 1972, p.15.

* It was a polyglot empire, a rummage-bag of an empire, united by neither common purpose in its creation, nor by language, race, religion, nor by strategic and economic design.'
  ibid., p.74.

* The British governing class saw the native races of the colonial empire, therefore, rather as old family tenants or cottagers; as a responsibility rather than as instruments of British power.'
  ibid., p.124

* 'It is a curious thought that, had the trade winds not blown from the Southeast, Australia could have been a continent settled and populated by Malays.'
  Gough Whitlam, Prime Minister of Australia, 1973.

* 'The Commonwealth [is] people meeting together, consulting, learning from each other, trying to persuade each other, and sometimes cooperating with each other, regardless of economics or geography, of ideology, or religion or race'. . . . 'It is not the existence or absence of joint action which justifies the Commonwealth. It is the fact of talking and of building upon a fact of history so as to further our mutual understanding.'
President Julius Nyerere, *Africa Digest,* Oct. 1973 pp.103-4.

Notes and References

Chapter 1. The Commonwealth

1. Dame Margery Perham, Introduction to Martin Wight, *The Development of the Legislative Council 1606-1945,* (Faber, 1946).
2. A comment made by L. S. Amery, former Colonial Secretary, (1924), quoted in Wight, *op. cit.,* p.136.
3. Sir Kenneth Wheare of Oxford University, a noted political scientist, proposed a formula which would allow member Commonwealth countries which were also republics to remain within the Commonwealth. The formula included the acceptance of the King as Head of the Commonwealth, a symbol of the free association of the members. The original form of words was derived from the preamble of the statute of Westminster, 1931.
4. H. Duncan Hall, *Commonwealth,* Van Nostrand 1971, ch. 7 gives many examples of such terminology.
5. The debate is discussed in J. D. B. Miller, 'South Africa's Departure', *Journal of Commonwealth Political Studies,* vol. 1, no. 1, and S. A. de Smith, 'The Commonwealth and South Africa', *University of Malaya Law Review,* vol. 3, no. 2.
6. Referring to the Commonwealth, the *Economist,* 6 June 1964, argued that 'while it endures, any member who quits injures himself more than anyone else'.
7. This declaration is printed in full in Appendix B.
8. M. Margaret Ball, *The Open Commonwealth,* Duke University Press, 1972, chapter 3.
9. C. E. Carrington, *The Liquidation of the British Empire,* Harrap, 1961.
10. Sir Andrew Cohen, *British Policy in Changing Africa,* Routledge, 1959.
11. D. A. Low and R. N. Pratt, *Buganda and British Overrule,* Oxford University Press, 1970.

Chapter 2. Empire into Commonwealth

1. Anonymous Cape Breton poet, quoted in M. Beloff, *Imperial Sunset,* vol. 1: *Britain's Liberal Empire 1897-1921,* Methuen, 1969, p.20
2. H. G. Wells, *Mr Britling Sees It Through,* Cassell, 1916, p.425
3. Kenneth E. Boulding and Tapan Mukerjee, 'Unprofitable Empire: Britain in India, 1800-1967, A Critique of the Hobson-Lenin Thesis on Imperialism. *Peace Research Society (International) Papers,* vol. 16, 1971 (the Rome Conference 1970), p.3.
4. Beloff, *op. cit.,* p.19, see, however, A. P. Thornton, *The Imperial Idea and its Enemies,* 1959. A shorter analysis is to be found in E. T. Stokes, *The Political Ideas of the English Imperialism,* Oxford University Press, 1960.
5. J. A. Cross, *Whitehall and the Commonwealth 1900-1966,* Routledge & Kegan Paul, 1967, *passim.*
6. K. E. Knorr, *British Colonial Theories, 1570-1850,* University of Toronto Press; Cass, 1967.
7. On Chatham see Sir Charles Grant Robertson, *Chatham and the British Empire,* 2nd edn, English Universities Press, 1970.
8. See R. Blake, *Disraeli,* Eyre & Spottiswoode, 1967. p.547.
9. Philip Mason, *Patterns of Dominance,* Oxford University Press, 1970.
10. See, for example, Frantz Fanon, *The Wretched of the Earth:* Macgibbon & Kee, 1965. 'In the colonial context the settler only ends his work of breaking in the native when the latter admits loudly and intelligibly the supremacy of the white man's values. In the period of decolonisation, the colonised masses mock at these very values, insult them and vomit them up.'
11. J. D. B. Miller, *Britain and the Old Dominions,* Chatto & Windus, 1966, pp. 15-17.
12. Brinley Thomas, *The Evolution of the Sterling Area and its Prospects,* in N. Mansergh, ed., *Commonwealth Perspectives* (Commonwealth Studies Center, Duke University), 1958.
13. J. Barzun, *Race, A Study in Superstition,* Harper, 1965.
14. J. H. Parry, *Europe and A Wider World 1415-1715,* Hutchinson, 1949, p.118. He recalls the saying of Governor Winthrop to the effect that there was no democracy in Israel.
15. ibid., p.191.
16. M. Wight, *The Development of the Legislative Council 1606-1945,* Faber, 1946, pp. 39-40.
17. Sir Ernest Barker, 'The Ideals of the Commonwealth', in Sydney D. Bailey, ed., *Parliamentary Government in the Commonwealth,* Hansard, 1951.

18. Hansard Society, 'Problems of Parliamentary Government in Colonies', *Parliamentary Affairs,* Winter 1952-53, pp.78-9.
19. Sir F.D. Lugard (later Lord Lugard), *The Dual Mandate in British Tropical Africa,* 1922.
20. The definition was drafted by Lord Balfour, British Prime Minister.
21. 22 Geo. 5, Chapter 4, See Sir Kenneth Wheare, *The Statute of Westminster and Dominion Status,* 5th edn., Oxford University Press, 1953.
22. Details of the Conference and its decision are given in *Keesings Contemporary Archives* vol. 1, 1931-34; pp.442-4.
23. Miller, *op. cit.,* pp.143-4.
24. Ronald Robinson, ed., *Developing the Third World,* Cambridge University Press, 1971, p.7.
25. *Economist,* 29 December 1973 – 4 January 1974, pp.54-5.

Chapter 3. The Old Countries of the Commonwealth

1. Michael Howard, *Encounter,* vol. 20, no. 1, Going into Europe, January, 1963, p.57.
2. J. D. B. Miller, *Britain and the Old Dominions,* Chatto & Windus, 1966, p.15.
3. E. M. Corbett, Quebec Confronts *Canada,* Oxford University Press, 1967.
4. The results of the Canadian elections of 30 October, 1972, are given in *Keesings Contemporary Archives.* 1973, p. 25891
5. O. H. K. Spate, *Australia,* Benn, 1968, p.103. Non Australians, particularly Americans, are puzzled by Australian culture and speech. 'The accent of the Australians,' says one of them, 'due to the elements from which their forebears came in England, most closely resembles the accent of the British lower class. However, their accent is no indication of their intelligence or ability and is actually quite interesting to listen to' [*sic*]. The New Zealanders on the other hand have an accent 'similar to that of the middle and upper class gentry of England': Harold C. Hinton, *The Far East and Southwest Pacific 1972,* The World Today Series, Washington, D.C., Stryker-Post Publications, pp. 11 and 62.
6. Miller *op.cit.,* p.73.
7. R. L. Watts, *New Federations, Experiments in the Commonwealth,* Oxford, Clarendon Press, 1965, pp.10-11. Indeed, Canadian and Australian (and American) federal types have been described as examples of 'cooperative federalism' in which the states or local units come to rely upon each other and, especially in financial matters, upon the federal or central authority.

See also David Soloman, *Australia's Government and Parliament,* Nelson 1973, chap 8.

8. The details of the Republican Referendum held on 5 October, 1960 are as follows:

	For Republic	Against Republic
Cape	271,418	269,784
Transvaal	406,632	325,041
Free State	110,171	33,438
Natal	42,299	135,598
South-West Africa	19,938	12,017
Total	850,458	775,878

Majority in favour of a Republic: 74,580
Total votes cast: 1,633,572

(Source: State of South Africa, *Year Book 1967,* p.48).

9. In 1961 the Prime Minister of the Union of South Africa, Dr H. F. Verwoerd, attended the Commonwealth Prime Ministers' Conference in London, contemplating an announcement that South Africa would soon declare itself a Republic on the model of India. Faced with considerable hostility from the African and Asian members of the Commonwealth, Verwoerd withdrew South Africa's application for continued membership of the Commonwealth and on 31 May, 1961, the Republic of South Africa was established outside the Commonwealth.

10. The extent of British investment in South Africa is discussed in *South African Connection,* by Christabel Gurney, Jonathan Steele and R. First, Temple Smith, 1972.

11. The text of the Statute of Westminster is given in Wheare, *op. cit.,* p.174.

12. Watts, *op. cit.,* p.34.

Chapter 4. The Commonwealth in Asia

1. Cited from *Quotations for Speakers and Writers,* ed. A. Andrews, Newnes, 1969.

2. Nicholas Mansergh, *Commonwealth Perspectives* (Duke University Press, 1958) p.31.

3. India alone, with about 550 million people comprises 60 per cent of the Commonwealth's population, and about 35 per cent of the total population in Asia are Commonwealth citizens.

4. R. Braibanti, 'Elite Cadres in the Bureaucracies of India, Pakistan, Ceylon and Malaya since Independence' in W. I. B. Hamilton, Kenneth Robinson and C. D. W. Goodwin, eds. *A Decade of the Commonwealth, 1955-1964,* Duke University Press, 1966, p.278.
5. Robert L. Hardgrave jr., *India, Government and Politics in a Developing Nation,* Harcourt Brace, 1970, chapter 7, The campaign for the election of 1967 was conducted 'in an atmosphere of frustration, despondency, uncertainty, and recurrent – almost continual – agitation.'
6. Mohandas Gandhi, *An Autobiography or the Story of My Experiments with Truth,* Ahmedabad, 1927; Joan V. Bondurant, *Conquest of Violence,* University of California Press, 1965; W. H. Morris-Jones, C. H. Philips, ed., *India's Political Idioms in Politics and Society in India,* Allen & Unwin, 1963, pp. 133-54.
7. Oscar Lewis, *Village Life in Northern India,* Vintage Books, 1965, p.149.
8. *The Times* (Special Supplement) 20 February, 1973.
9. K. Callard, *Pakistan: a political study,* Allen & Unwin, 1958.
10. Neville Maxwell, *India's China War,* Cape, 1970, p.11.
11. J. M. Gullick, *Malaysia and its Neighbours,* World Studies Series, Routledge & Kegan Paul, 1967.
12. R. L. Watts, *New Federations, Experiments in the Commonwealth,* Oxford, Clarendon Press, 1965.
13. Hansard Society, 'Problems of Parliamentary Government in Colonies.' *Parliamentary Affairs,* vol. 6, no. 1, Winter 1952-53.
14. R. S. Milne, 'Political modernisation, Malaysia', *Journal of Commonwealth Political Studies,* vol. vii, 1969, pp.7-19.
15. G. P. Means, *Malaysian Politics,* University of London Press, 1970, chapter 21, for a suggestion that in Malaya most of the population has as yet not started to think 'in terms of loyalty to a political entity which is Malaysia'.
16. for details of the minor parties and of the election as a whole, see David Hawkins and Stuart Drummond, 'The Malaysian elections of 1969: crisis for the alliance', *The World Today,* September 1969.
17. Means, *op. cit.,* p.366.
18. Chan Heng Chee, *Singapore, the Politics of Survival 1965-1967,* Oxford in Asia, 1971, p.10.
19. Gullick, *op. cit.,* p.19.
20. For further details see, P. B. Harris, 'The international future of Hong Kong', *International Affairs,* Royal Institute of International Affairs, January 1972, pp. 60-71.
21. See Philip Mason, *Patterns of Dominance,* Oxford University Press for Institute of Race Relations, 1971, p.85.

Chapter 5. The Commonwealth in Africa

1. K. A. Busia, *Africa in Search of Democracy,* Routledge & Kegan Paul, 1967, pp. 115-16.
2. D. Apter, *The Gold Coast in Transition,* Princeton University Press, 1955; D. Austin, *Politics in Ghana, 1946-1960,* Oxford University Press; W. Arthur Lewis, *Politics in West Africa,* Allen & Unwin.
3. Robert W. July, *A History of the African People,* Faber 1970, chapter 15.
4. Quoted in Edward Luttwak, *Coup d'Etat,* Penguin Books, 1970; p.169; see also Robert Pinkney, *Ghana under Military Rule,* 1966-1969, Methuen, 1972.
5. Victor A. Olorunsola, ed., *The Politics of Cultural Sub-Nationalism in Africa,* Doubleday, Anchor Books, 1972, p.12.
6. See Donald S. Rothchild, *Toward Unity in Africa: a study of federalism in British Africa,* Washington, Public Affairs Press, 1960, p.142.
7. Royal Institute of International Affairs, *Survey of International Affairs 1959-60,* ch. 7, and ibid, *1961,* ch. 8.
8. On the Biafra episode see *Africa Contemporary Record, Annual Survey and Documents, 1968-69,* London, Rex Collings, pp. 645-89.
9. See P. B. Harris, *Studies in African Politics,* Hutchinson, 1970, pp.71-6 for an estimate of the place of the Rhodesian issue in Commonwealth politics.
10. Harris, *op. cit.,* pp. 127-31.
11. See Lewis H. Gann, 'Rhodesia and the prophets', *African Affairs,* April 1972, p.19, for an appraisal of the prophecies made regarding Rhodesia's chances of survival during the period 1965-72.
12. July, *op cit.,* p.506.
13. D. A. Low and R. C. Pratt, *Buganda and British Overrule, 1900-1955,* Oxford University Press, 1970.
14. July, *op. cit.,* p.409.
15. Neslon Kasfir, 'Cultural sub-nationalism in Uganda', in Olorunsola, *op. cit.,* ch. 2, p.53.
16. Walter Elkan, *The Economic Development of Uganda,* Oxford University Press, 1961, p.13.
17. July, *op. cit.,* pp. 410-12.
18. C. G. Rosberg and J. Nottingham, *The Myth of Mau Mau: nationalism in Kenya,* Praeger, 1966.
19. Donald Rothchild, 'Ethnic inequalities in Kenya', in Olorunsola, *op. cit.,* ch. 5, p.307.
20. *Africa Contemporary Record: Annual Survey and Documents 1971-1972,* Rex Collings, pp. [B] 213-15.

21. P. B. Harris, *The Withdrawal of the Major European Powers from Africa,* University College of Rhodesia, Monographs in Political Science no. 2, 1969.
22. Richard Pares, 'The revolt against colonialism', in *The Historian's Business and other essays,* Oxford University Press, 1961, p.79.
23. Basil Davidson, *Can Africa Survive?* Heinemann, 1975. p. 145.

Chapter 6. Conclusion

1. Anthony Sampson, *Anatomy of Britain,* Hodder & Stoughton, 1962.
2. L. P. Mair, *Australia in New Guinea,* 2nd edn., Melbourne University Press, 1970.
3. H. Victor Wiseman, *Britain and the Commonwealth,* Allen & Unwin, 1965, p.73.
4. A. A. Afrifa, *The Ghana Coup,* Cass, 1966, pp. 51-2.

Bibliography

These books may be helpful in further reading on the subject.

Beloff, M., *Imperial Sunset,* Volume I, Britain's Liberal Empire, 1897-1921 (Methuen).

Keith, Sir Arthur Berriedale, *Speeches and Documents on the British Dominions,* 1918-1931, (Oxford University Press), 1931.

Mansergh, N. (ed.), *Documents and Speeches on British Commonwealth Affairs* (Oxford University Press) 1963.

Mansergh, N., *The Commonwealth Experience* Weidenfeld (1969).

Marshall Geoffrey, *Parliamentary Sovereignty and the Commonwealth* (Oxford University Press) 1957.

Miller, J.D.B., *Survey of Commonwealth Affairs,* Problems of Expansion and Attrition, 1953-69, (Oxford University Press) (published for the Royal Institute of International Affairs) 1974.

Wheare, Sir Kenneth, *The Constitutional Structure of the Commonwealth* (Oxford, At the Clarendon Press), 1960.

Wight, Martin, *The Development and the Legislative Council, 1606-1945* (Faber), 1947.

Index

This index is in three parts:
A – Places *B – Persons*
C – Ideas

A. Places

B. Persons

C. Ideas